Certification Study Companion Series

The Apress Certification Study Companion Series offers guidance and hands-on practice to support technical and business professionals who are studying for an exam in the pursuit of an industry certification. Professionals worldwide seek to achieve certifications in order to advance in a career role, reinforce knowledge in a specific discipline, or to apply for or change jobs. This series focuses on the most widely taken certification exams in a given field. It is designed to be user friendly, tracking to topics as they appear in a given exam and work alongside other certification material as professionals prepare for their exam.

More information about this series at `https://link.springer.com/bookseries/17100`.

Azure Data Fundamentals Certification Companion

A Complete Guide to DP-900 Exam Success

Naveen Kumar M

apress®

Azure Data Fundamentals Certification Companion: A Complete Guide to DP-900 Exam Success

Naveen Kumar M
Chennai, Tamil Nadu, India

ISBN-13 (pbk): 979-8-8688-1683-3 ISBN-13 (electronic): 979-8-8688-1684-0
https://doi.org/10.1007/979-8-8688-1684-0

Copyright © 2025 by Naveen Kumar M

This work is subject to copyright. All rights are reserved by the Publisher, whether the whole or part of the material is concerned, specifically the rights of translation, reprinting, reuse of illustrations, recitation, broadcasting, reproduction on microfilms or in any other physical way, and transmission or information storage and retrieval, electronic adaptation, computer software, or by similar or dissimilar methodology now known or hereafter developed.

Trademarked names, logos, and images may appear in this book. Rather than use a trademark symbol with every occurrence of a trademarked name, logo, or image we use the names, logos, and images only in an editorial fashion and to the benefit of the trademark owner, with no intention of infringement of the trademark.

The use in this publication of trade names, trademarks, service marks, and similar terms, even if they are not identified as such, is not to be taken as an expression of opinion as to whether or not they are subject to proprietary rights.

While the advice and information in this book are believed to be true and accurate at the date of publication, neither the authors nor the editors nor the publisher can accept any legal responsibility for any errors or omissions that may be made. The publisher makes no warranty, express or implied, with respect to the material contained herein.

>
> Managing Director, Apress Media LLC: Welmoed Spahr
> Acquisitions Editor: Smriti Srivastava
> Desk Editor: Laura Berendson
> Editorial Project Manager: Jessica Vakili

Cover image from Pixabay.com

Distributed to the book trade worldwide by Springer Science+Business Media New York, 1 New York Plaza, New York, NY 10004. Phone 1-800-SPRINGER, fax (201) 348-4505, e-mail orders-ny@springer-sbm.com, or visit www.springeronline.com. Apress Media, LLC is a Delaware LLC and the sole member (owner) is Springer Science + Business Media Finance Inc (SSBM Finance Inc). SSBM Finance Inc is a **Delaware** corporation.

For information on translations, please e-mail booktranslations@springernature.com; for reprint, paperback, or audio rights, please e-mail bookpermissions@springernature.com.

Apress titles may be purchased in bulk for academic, corporate, or promotional use. eBook versions and licenses are also available for most titles. For more information, reference our Print and eBook Bulk Sales web page at http://www.apress.com/bulk-sales.

Any source code or other supplementary material referenced by the author in this book is available to readers on the Github repository: https://github.com/Apress/Azure-Data-Fundamentals-Certification-Companion. For more detailed information, please visit https://www.apress.com/gp/services/source-code.

If disposing of this product, please recycle the paper

To the one who stood by me with love and patience – my wife.

Table of Contents

About the Author xiii

About the Technical Reviewer xv

Acknowledgments xvii

Introduction xix

Chapter 1: Exam Overview and Structure 1

Introduction to DP-900 Certification 2

    Purpose of the Exam 2

    What Is the Primary Purpose of the DP-900 Exam? 2

    Who Should Take This Exam? 3

    Benefits of DP-900 Certification 4

Exam Domains and Weightage 6

    Understanding Core Data Concepts (25–30%) 7

    Working with Relational Data on Azure (20–25%) 8

    Exploring Non-relational Data on Azure (15–20%) 8

    Analytics Workloads on Azure (25–30%) 9

Understanding the Exam Format 10

    DP-900 Question Types 10

    Time Allocation and Scoring System 11

Study Plan and Strategies 12

    Four-Week Preparation Plan 12

    Week 1: Chapter 2 – Understanding Core Data Concepts (25–30%) 12

    Week 2: Chapter 3 – Working with Relational Data on Azure (20–25%) 13

TABLE OF CONTENTS

    Week 3: Chapter 4 – Exploring Non-relational Data on Azure (15–20%) 13

    Week 4: Chapter 5 – Analytics Workloads on Azure (25–30%) 14

    Leveraging Microsoft Learn, Documentation, and Practice Labs 14

Summary 15

    1. Introduction to DP-900 Certification 16

    2. Exam Domains and Weightage 16

    3. Understanding the Exam Format 17

    4. Study Plan and Strategies 18

Chapter 2: Understanding Core Data Concepts 19

Introduction to Data Representation 20

    Overview 20

    Ways to Represent Data 20

    Structured Data 21

    Semi-structured Data 24

    Unstructured Data 27

Data Storage Options 29

    Delimited Text Files 30

    Key Characteristics 30

    Example 31

    JavaScript Object Notation (JSON) 32

    JSON Structure 33

    Extensible Markup Language (XML) 34

    Binary Large Object (BLOB) 36

    Optimized File Formats 37

Explore Databases 39

    Relational Databases 39

    Non-relational Databases 40

TABLE OF CONTENTS

Data Workloads 41
    Transactional Workloads 42
    Online Transaction Processing (OLTP) 42
    Analytical Workloads 44
    Online Analytical Processing (OLAP) 44
    Key Differences Between Transactional and Analytical Workloads 48
Roles and Responsibilities in Data Workloads 49
    1. Database Administrator (DBA) 50
    2. Data Engineer 50
    3. Data Analyst 51
Explore Data Services 52
    Data Services in Azure 52
    Roles and Services 56
Summary 57

Chapter 3: Working with Relational Data on Azure 61

Relational Data Concepts 62
    Features of Relational Data 62
    Explore SQL 70
    Explore Database 76
Azure Relational Data Services 81
    Overview 81
    Azure SQL Family 81
    Comparison of Azure SQL Services 82
    Key Features of Azure SQL Services 83
    Business Benefits of Azure Relational Data Services 84
    Comparative Business Benefits Summary 87

TABLE OF CONTENTS

Open Source Relational Databases on Azure 89
    Overview of Services 89
    Azure Managed Open Source Database Services 90
    Benefits of Azure Managed Open Source Databases 92
Summary 94

Chapter 4: Exploring Non-relational Data on Azure 97

Introduction to Non-relational Data 98
    Overview 98
    Non-relational Data 99
    Why Non-relational on Azure? 99
    Difference Between Relational and Non-relational Data 100
    When to Choose Non-relational Data? 101
    Examples of Non-relational Data 101
Azure Storage Services 103
    Explore Azure Blob Storage 103
    Explore Azure Data Lake Storage Gen2 107
    Explore Microsoft OneLake in Fabric 111
    Explore Azure File Storage 115
    Explore Azure Tables 119
Azure Cosmos DB: A Multi-model Database Service 122
    Explore Azure Cosmos DB: Key Features and When to Use 122
    Explore APIs for Azure Cosmos DB 125
    Common Use Cases for Azure Cosmos DB 129
Summary 133
    1. Non-relational vs. Relational Data 133
    2. Azure Storage Services for Non-relational Data 133
    3. Azure Cosmos DB: The Multi-model Database Powerhouse 134
    4. Real-World Applications of Azure Cosmos DB 135

Chapter 5: Analytics Workloads on Azure 137

Explore Fundamentals of Large-Scale Analytics..138
    Describe Data Warehousing Architecture 138
    Explore Data Ingestion Pipelines 141
    Explore Analytical Data Stores..146

Explore Fundamentals of Real-Time Analytics...151
    Understand Batch and Stream Processing..151
    Core Components of a Stream Processing Architecture.............................159
    Explore Microsoft Fabric Real-Time Intelligence...163
    Explore Apache Spark Structured Streaming 166

Explore Fundamentals of Data Visualization with Microsoft Power BI.............169
    Introduction 169
    Capabilities and Features of Power BI..170

Building Data Models in Power BI..174
    Understanding Analytical Models 174
    Tables and Schema Design 175
    Attribute Hierarchies..176
    Data Modeling in Microsoft Power BI 177

Choosing the Right Visualization for Insights..178
    Key Considerations for Data Visualization 178
    Common Visualization Types in Power BI 179
    Interactive Reports in Power BI 181

Summary..182
    1. Explore Fundamentals of Large-Scale Analytics 182
    2. Explore Fundamentals of Real-Time Data Analytics...............................183
    3. Explore Fundamentals of Data Visualization with Microsoft Power BI 184

TABLE OF CONTENTS

Chapter 6: Exam Preparation and Practice 185
Overview 185
Online vs. Offline Exam Readiness.. 185
    Online Exam Readiness (Remote Proctored Exam) 186
    Offline Exam Readiness (Test Center–Based Exam)..................................... 187
    Exam Tips and Common Pitfalls 189
Final Preparation Checklist 191
After the Exam 191
Practice Questions and Answers.. 192
    Practice Questions with Explanations 192
    Scenario-Based Practice Questions 203
Mock Exam 208
    Full-Length Practice Test... 208
    Answers and Explanations 221
Conclusion 225

Index 227

About the Author

Naveen Kumar is an accomplished IT professional with more than 14 years of experience specializing in data engineering and cloud technologies. He has extensive expertise in database design, data warehousing, ETL development, and data-driven solution architecture. With a strong background in data modeling, visualization, and scalable system design, he has successfully delivered solutions that address complex business challenges.

As a passionate technical writer, mentor, and speaker, Naveen actively shares his knowledge through articles, webinars, YouTube content, and community engagements. With a self-driven, results-oriented approach, he continuously explores emerging technologies, contributing to innovative solutions that drive business success.

About the Technical Reviewer

Dr. Gomathi S is a dedicated educator, author, and technology trainer with over 14 years of experience empowering students, developers, and professionals in the fields of software development, data analytics, and artificial intelligence. Her areas of expertise include Microsoft Power BI, Business Central, Copilot Studio, Power Apps, Python, Tableau, and machine learning.

With a Ph.D. in computer science specializing in data mining, she brings both academic rigor and real-world practicality to her teaching. Dr. Gomathi is widely recognized for her hands-on, example-driven training style, making complex technical topics accessible and actionable for learners at all levels.

She has authored multiple technical books and research papers and has filed several national and international patents. Her deep involvement in the tech education community includes designing curriculum, conducting workshops, and creating digital learning content across platforms and development environments.

Through her commitment to democratizing access to AI-powered tools like Business Central and Copilot Studio, she continues to inspire learners to embrace intelligent development and build future-ready skills.

Acknowledgments

To my wife, Priya (Shanthi Priya N) – the one who stood beside me when the pages were blank. My greatest supporter, my truest friend. Your unwavering strength, love, and patience made this journey possible, and for that, I am forever grateful.

I extend my heartfelt thanks to Dr. Gomathi S, a mentor whose belief in me and encouragement helped bring this book to completion. Your trust, encouragement, and unwavering support were constant sources of motivation.

To Susmi Jose – no words can truly express my gratitude. You've been my constant support, guiding me like a mentor, standing by me like a friend. You always believed in me at every step, encouraging me to keep moving forward.

To my friend Ramanathan A, who once told me I should write a book, not necessarily a technical one – thank you for supporting my writing journey from the very start. This book is the result of the seed you planted.

Finally, to Shobana Srinivasan and Smriti Srivastava – your consistent support and keen insights throughout every stage, from proposal to publication, were truly indispensable.

To all of you – your encouragement, belief, and love have made this journey possible. Thank you for helping me bring this dream to life.

Introduction

In the era of data-driven decision-making, organizations across every industry are harnessing the power of data to gain actionable insights, enhance operational efficiency, and fuel innovation. As cloud adoption accelerates, Microsoft Azure has emerged as a leading platform for data services, offering scalable, secure, and versatile tools for data storage, processing, and analytics. With businesses increasingly relying on these tools, a foundational understanding of Azure's data services is becoming essential for both technical and non-technical professionals.

Azure Data Fundamentals Certification Companion: A Complete Guide to DP-900 Exam Success is your comprehensive resource for building that foundation and achieving success in the DP-900 certification exam. This book is carefully designed to provide learners with a deep yet approachable understanding of core data concepts and how they are implemented in Azure.

Whether you're an aspiring data professional, a student, a business analyst, or an IT generalist seeking to expand your knowledge of cloud data technologies, this guide will equip you with the concepts and practical insights needed to confidently take the next step in your cloud learning journey.

Throughout this book, we will explore the key domains of the DP-900 exam, starting with fundamental data principles – such as relational and non-relational data types, batch vs. stream processing, and data analytics workloads. You'll then dive into how Azure implements these concepts using services like Azure SQL Database, Cosmos DB, Azure Data Lake, Synapse Analytics, and Power BI.

INTRODUCTION

Each chapter is aligned with the official DP-900 exam objectives, helping you build both theoretical understanding and practical awareness. With clear explanations, real-world examples, and chapter-wise review questions, this book ensures you not only prepare thoroughly for the exam but also develop a meaningful grasp of how data solutions function in modern cloud environments.

We also dedicate a section to exam readiness strategies, including tips, mock questions, and insights, to help reduce anxiety and maximize your chances of success on exam day.

Whether you're just beginning your journey into the world of data or you're pivoting your career toward cloud-based roles, this book will serve as your trusted guide. By the time you complete it, you'll have built a solid data fundamentals knowledge base and be well prepared to earn your Microsoft Certified: Azure Data Fundamentals credential.

Start your learning journey with confidence, and take the first step toward becoming a data-savvy professional in the cloud era. Your success in the DP-900 exam and beyond begins here.

CHAPTER 1

Exam Overview and Structure

In this chapter, you will learn about the form and substance of the DP-900: Microsoft Azure Data Fundamentals question test. This core exam validates the candidate's knowledge of common data concepts and how they are implemented using Microsoft Azure data services. You will learn the objectives and advantages of certification and who this certification is intended for.

We'll then dissect the core domains of the test, such as relational and non-relational data and analytics workloads. You will familiarize yourself with how the test is structured, what kinds of questions you can expect, and how it's scored. Lastly, we'll give you a complete study plan and the top resources to study effectively.

You will be clear about what to learn, how this course is structured, and what strategy you should follow to prepare for and pass the DP-900 exam so that you can break ground on Azure data-related certifications.

CHAPTER 1   EXAM OVERVIEW AND STRUCTURE

Introduction to DP-900 Certification

Purpose of the Exam

DP-900: Microsoft Azure Data Fundamentals certification exams are intended to evaluate proficiency in understanding the following core data concepts and being able to work within the Microsoft Azure environment. This is a good certificate if you have started in the data field or if you have data responsibilities in your current job but don't have a strong technical background. This exam is intended to test the candidates' knowledge of the different types of data stores, both relational and non-relational, and what options are available with each on Azure.

What Is the Primary Purpose of the DP-900 Exam?

- Concepts pertaining to data and data storage; core data concepts, such as data types and data processing

- The concepts of relational data and how it is implemented in Azure using services like Azure SQL Database and Azure Synapse Analytics

- Non-relational data concepts and how to use Microsoft Azure services to support these, for example, Azure Cosmos DB and Azure Blob Storage

- Analytical workloads and how to govern and optimize them with Azure services such as Azure Data Lake, Azure Databricks, and Azure Synapse Analytics

CHAPTER 1   EXAM OVERVIEW AND STRUCTURE

By passing the DP-900 exam, candidates demonstrate their ability to work with data in the cloud, understand the different types of data storage and processing options available on Azure, and make informed decisions about which services to use for specific scenarios.

Who Should Take This Exam?

The DP-900 exam is intended for everybody, whether they are a data engineer or not, from a variety of professionals engaged in work related to data. This exam is especially ideal for

- **New to Data Engineering**: For those new to data engineering looking to gain a solid foundation of data concepts and services in Azure.

- **IT Professionals**: IT professionals who work with data as a part of their job but do not possess a technical data engineering background.

- **Database Administrators**: Database administrators wanting to learn about cloud-based data services and how to use them to manage and process data.

- **Data Analysts**: It would be suitable for data analysts who would like to know about the core data infrastructure and how analytics is performed there.

- **Students and Career Changers**: With or without a job but interested in a career in data or data-related fields and want to start with a certification that introduces the basics.

The DP-900 exam also serves as a prerequisite to more enhanced Azure certifications as shown in Figure 1-1.

CHAPTER 1   EXAM OVERVIEW AND STRUCTURE

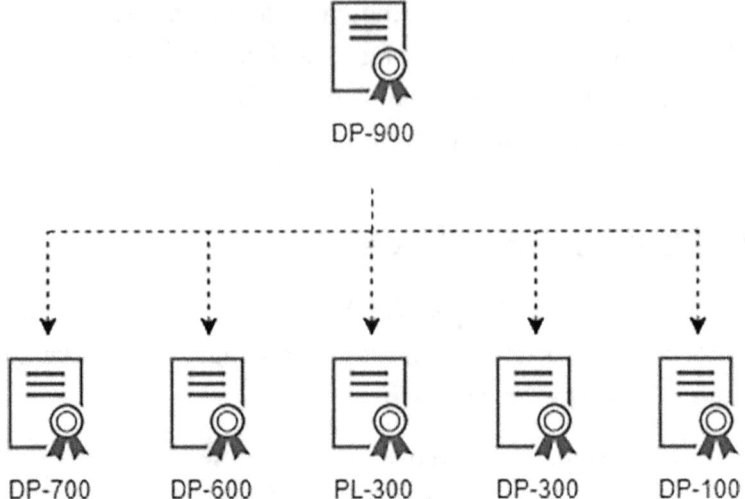

Figure 1-1. *Azure Data Certification Flow*

- DP-700 (Microsoft Fabric Data Engineer Associate)
- DP-600 (Microsoft Fabric Analytics Engineer Associate)
- PL-300 (Power BI Data Analyst Associate)
- DP-300 (Azure Database Administrator Associate)
- DP-100 (Azure Data Scientist Associate)

It provides a solid foundation for those who plan to pursue these higher-level certifications in the future.

Benefits of DP-900 Certification

Here's why it's beneficial to earn a DP-900 credential for both emerging tech pros and their companies:

1. **Foundational Knowledge Validation**: The certification validates an understanding of basic data concepts and how they are implemented in Azure. This is a must-know for anyone who works with data in the cloud.

2. **Career Opportunities**: The DP-900 certification helps open new doors to prospective jobs in data analysis, data engineering, and database administration. It shows an employer that you possess the core skills required to work with data in the cloud.

3. **Increased Earning Potential**: Many certified professionals receive more than their non-certified counterparts. Earning the DP-900 certification could help you differentiate yourself in a crowded job market and increase your earning potential.

4. **Benefits to the Organization**: Organizations benefit from having employees with the DP-900 certification, as it builds a strong foundation in cloud data management. This can result in better utilization of Azure data services and more informed storage and processing decisions.

5. **Prepare for Advanced Certifications**: If you have plans to take more advanced Azure certifications, then DP-900 is the ideal beginning. It is the prerequisite for learning some other hard topics about data engineering and database administration.

6. **Microsoft Resources Certification:** Certified professionals have access to Microsoft resources, such as training and community support options, freeing up more time to spend on other teaching tasks. These resources can help you keep current on the newest Azure data services and keep your skills current.

Exam Domains and Weightage

The DP-900 exam breaks down into four main areas, which span different areas of data concepts and Azure data services. The domains are also weighted differently according to their relative importance to the examination. Knowing the percentage of questions in each of these areas will allow you to budget your time for the different parts of the test and, more importantly, make sure you study the right bits.

Table 1-1. Exam Domain and Weightage

Domain	Weightage
Understanding Core Data Concepts	25–30%
Working with Relational Data on Azure	20–25%
Exploring Non-relational Data on Azure	15–20%
Analytics Workloads on Azure	25–30%

Table 1-1 shows an overview of the key areas covered in the exam. Each domain is explained in detail in the sections that follow.

CHAPTER 1   EXAM OVERVIEW AND STRUCTURE

Understanding Core Data Concepts (25–30%)

The first domain is Understanding Core Data Concepts. This testing domain carries the most weight in the test, making up 25–30% of all of the questions. This domain includes material that is prerequisite to working with data in all settings, from on-premises to the cloud. Some of the topics in this area are

- **Data Types and Structures**: Understanding the different types of data (structured, semi-structured, and unstructured) and the way they are being stored and processed

- **Data Storage**: Knowledge of different data store options such as databases, data warehouses, and data lakes

- **Data Processing**: An understanding of data processing, including batch and real time

- **Data Security and Compliance**: Understanding data security fundamentals, including encryption, access control, and regulatory compliance

This domain is especially important as it serves as the basis of the others. It will be almost impossible to understand more advanced exam topics without a good understanding of fundamental data concepts.

CHAPTER 1   EXAM OVERVIEW AND STRUCTURE

Working with Relational Data on Azure (20–25%)

The second domain, Working with Relational Data on Azure, makes up 20–25% of the test. This area covers relational data concepts and how they are used in Azure. Topics in this domain include

- **Relational Database Concepts**: Understanding the basics of relational databases, including tables, rows, columns, and relationships between tables
- **Azure SQL Database**: Familiarity with Azure SQL Database, a fully managed relational database service in Azure
- **Azure Synapse Analytics**: Knowledge of Azure Synapse Analytics, a service that combines big data and data warehousing capabilities
- **Data Migration**: Learn how to migrate on-premises relational databases to Azure, including Azure Database Migration Service

This domain is relevant to anyone who deals with relational data and covers the main Azure services for managing and processing relational data in the cloud.

Exploring Non-relational Data on Azure (15–20%)

The third domain, "Exploring Non-relational Data on Azure," accounts for 15–20% of the exam. This domain covers non-relational data concepts and how they are implemented in Azure. Topics in this domain include

- **Non-relational Database Concepts**: Understanding the basics of non-relational databases, including document stores, key-value stores, and graph databases

- **Azure Cosmos DB**: Familiarity with Azure Cosmos DB, a globally distributed, multi-model database service

- **Azure Blob Storage**: Understanding of Azure Blob Storage, a service to store large volumes of unstructured data

- **Data Modeling for Non-relational Data**: Learn how to model your data for NoSQL databases, including denormalization and partitioning

This is a critical domain area for anyone working with non-relational data, considering this comprises the primary Azure services for non-relational data management and processing in the cloud.

Analytics Workloads on Azure (25–30%)

The fourth domain, Analytics Workloads on Azure, has a percentage weight of 25–30%. This domain pertains to analytics topics and the application of analytics in an Azure environment. Topics in this domain include

- **Data Analytics Concepts**: Understanding the basics of data analytics, including descriptive, diagnostic, predictive, and prescriptive analytics

- **Azure Data Lake**: Knowledge of Azure Data Lake, which is a scalable data storage and analytic service

- **Azure Databricks**: Understanding of Azure Databricks for big data analytics and machine learning

CHAPTER 1   EXAM OVERVIEW AND STRUCTURE

- **Azure Synapse Analytics**: Discover how to use Azure Synapse Analytics for big data and data warehousing needs
- **Data Visualization**: Familiarity with data visualization tools, such as Power BI, and how to use them to generate data insights

This domain is important for anyone who works with analytics, as it covers the key Azure services used to manage and process analytics workloads in the cloud.

Understanding the Exam Format

The DP-900 is focused on testing your knowledge about data workloads and Azure data services via different question types. Knowing how the exam is structured can make your prepping more efficient and can give you the needed structure while taking the exam.

DP-900 Question Types

The DP-900 exam includes several types of questions, each designed to test different aspects of your knowledge. These question types are summarized in Table 1-2.

CHAPTER 1　EXAM OVERVIEW AND STRUCTURE

Table 1-2. Question Types and Examples

Question Type	Description	Example
Multiple Choice	These are the most common type of questions on the exam. You will be presented with a question and several possible answers, and you will need to select the correct answer(s). Some questions may have more than one correct answer, so be sure to read the instructions carefully	Selecting one or more correct Azure services for a given scenario
Drag-and-Drop	These questions require dragging and dropping items into correct positions. Often involve matching concepts or ordering steps in a process	You may be asked to match Azure services to their corresponding use cases or to arrange steps in a process in the correct order
Case Studies	Case study questions present you with a scenario and ask you to answer questions based on the information provided. These questions are designed to test your ability to apply your knowledge to real-world situations	Analyzing a business problem and recommending suitable Azure data services based on provided details

Time Allocation and Scoring System

The DP-900 exam consists of 40–60 questions, and you will have 60 minutes to complete the exam. The exact number of questions may vary, but you can expect to answer around 40–60 questions in total.

11

CHAPTER 1   EXAM OVERVIEW AND STRUCTURE

The exam is scored on a scale of 1–1000, with a minimum passing score of 700. The scoring is determined by the difficulty of the questions, with harder ones being worth more points. There is no negative score for incorrect answers, but be sure you have answered all the questions.

To manage your time effectively during the exam, it is recommended that you spend no more than 1–1.5 minutes on each question. If you encounter a difficult question, mark it for review and move on to the next question. You can return to the marked questions at the end of the exam if you have time.

Study Plan and Strategies

Preparing for the DP-900 exam requires a well-structured study plan and the right resources. In this section, we will outline a four-week preparation plan and discuss the best resources for exam success.

Four-Week Preparation Plan

A four-week preparation plan is ideal for most candidates, as it provides enough time to cover all the exam domains without feeling rushed.

Here is a suggested study plan.

Week 1: Chapter 2 – Understanding Core Data Concepts (25–30%)

- **Day 1-2**: Study structured, semi-structured, and unstructured data types, including use cases for each.
- **Day 3-4**: Learn about file storage formats like JSON, CSV, and Parquet, and understand optimized file formats.

CHAPTER 1   EXAM OVERVIEW AND STRUCTURE

- **Day 5-6**: Explore relational and non-relational databases, and understand the differences between them.
- **Day 7**: Review transactional and analytical workloads and their key differences.

Week 2: Chapter 3 – Working with Relational Data on Azure (20–25%)

- **Day 1-2**: Study relational data features, normalization, SQL basics, and database objects.
- **Day 3-4**: Learn about the Azure SQL Family – Azure SQL Database, Managed Instance, and SQL Server on VMs.
- **Day 5-6**: Explore open source relational databases on Azure – MySQL, PostgreSQL, and MariaDB.
- **Day 7**: Review Azure-managed open source database services and their benefits.

Week 3: Chapter 4 – Exploring Non-relational Data on Azure (15–20%)

- **Day 1-2**: Understand non-relational data and how it differs from relational data, with practical examples.
- **Day 3-4**: Learn about Azure Blob Storage, Data Lake Gen2, OneLake in Fabric, and other storage services.

- **Day 5–6**: Explore Cosmos DB, including its multi-model support, APIs, and key use cases.
- **Day 7**: Study data modeling approaches for non-relational data and review the week's topics.

Week 4: Chapter 5 – Analytics Workloads on Azure (25–30%)

- **Day 1–2**: Study data analytics concepts and data warehousing architecture, including Azure Synapse Analytics.
- **Day 3–4**: Learn about data ingestion pipelines using Azure Data Factory and explore analytics data stores.
- **Day 5–6**: Understand batch vs. stream processing, real-time intelligence with Microsoft Fabric, and Apache Spark structured streaming.
- **Day 7**: Explore Power BI capabilities, build data models, and learn how to choose the right visualization for insights.

Leveraging Microsoft Learn, Documentation, and Practice Labs

Microsoft offers a wealth of resources to help you prepare for the DP-900 exam. These resources include

1. **Microsoft Learn**: Microsoft Learn is free and interactive and offers courses designed for the DP-900 exam. These modules are designed to cover all of the exam domains and feature hands-on labs giving you the opportunity to practice with Azure data services.

2. **Microsoft Documentation**: The official Microsoft documentation provides in-depth information on all Azure data services. It is a valuable resource for understanding the features and capabilities of each service.

3. **Practice Labs**: Hands-on experience is essential for passing the DP-900 exam. Microsoft Learn offers practice labs that allow you to work with Azure data services in a real-world environment. These labs are a great way to reinforce your knowledge and gain practical experience.

By following a structured study plan and leveraging the right resources, you can increase your chances of passing the DP-900 exam and earning your Azure Data Fundamentals certification.

Summary

In this chapter, we explored the DP-900 Azure Data Fundamentals certification exam in detail, providing a comprehensive guide to help you understand its purpose, structure, and preparation strategies. Here's a summary of the key points covered.

CHAPTER 1   EXAM OVERVIEW AND STRUCTURE

1. Introduction to DP-900 Certification

- The DP-900 exam validates foundational knowledge of core data concepts and Azure data services, making it ideal for beginners and professionals working with data.

- **Who Should Take This Exam?** The certification is tailored for beginners in data engineering, IT professionals, database administrators, data analysts, students, and career changers. It also serves as a stepping stone for advanced certifications like the DP-700 (Microsoft Fabric Data Engineer Associate).

- **Benefits of Certification**: Earning the DP-900 certification validates foundational data skills, enhances career opportunities, increases earning potential, and prepares candidates for advanced Azure certifications.

2. Exam Domains and Weightage

The DP-900 exam is divided into four domains, each with a specific weightage:

1. **Understanding Core Data Concepts (25–30%)**: Covers data types, storage options, processing techniques, and data security

2. **Working with Relational Data on Azure (20–25%)**: Focuses on relational database concepts, Azure SQL Database, Azure Synapse Analytics, and data migration

3. **Exploring Non-relational Data on Azure (15–20%)**: Explores non-relational data concepts, Azure Cosmos DB, Azure Blob Storage, and data modeling

4. **Analytics Workloads on Azure (25–30%)**: Includes data analytics concepts, Azure Data Lake, Azure Databricks, Azure Synapse Analytics, and data visualization tools like Power BI

Understanding the weightage of each domain helps candidates allocate study time effectively.

3. Understanding the Exam Format

- The DP-900 exam consists of 40–60 questions to be completed in 60 minutes.

- **Question Types:** Multiple choice, drag-and-drop, and case study questions are used to assess knowledge and practical application.

- **Scoring System:** The exam is scored on a scale of 1–1000, with a passing score of 700. No penalties are applied for incorrect answers, so it's better to attempt all questions.

- **Time Management:** Allocate 1–1.5 minutes per question and mark difficult questions for review to ensure efficient time usage.

4. Study Plan and Strategies

- A **four-week preparation plan** is recommended to cover all exam domains systematically:
    - Week 1: Core Data Concepts
    - Week 2: Relational Data on Azure
    - Week 3: Non-relational Data on Azure
    - Week 4: Analytics Workloads on Azure
- **Key Resources**: Leverage Microsoft Learn, official documentation, and practice labs for hands-on experience.
- **Additional Resources**: Use books, online courses, practice exams, and study groups to reinforce knowledge and identify areas for improvement.

CHAPTER 2

Understanding Core Data Concepts

In this chapter, you will get introduced to the basic concepts of data representation and how data can be organized in various formats. You will discover types of data, for example, structured, semi-structured, and unstructured data, with examples and use cases. The chapter also walks through the options available for data storage, explaining the details of various data formats, such as JSON and CSV, as well as optimized file formats such as Avro, ORC, and Parquet and other storage services provided by Azure.

Next, you will take a look at the two general classes of data workloads: transactional workloads and analytical workloads. By knowing their definitions, characteristics, and main differences, you will be able to tell when to use which approach according to your needs.

Lastly, the chapter introduces the different roles and responsibilities involved in data workloads: Database Administrator, Data Engineer, and Data Analyst. You will explore the tasks and tools that fall under each role and gain insight into how each role will contribute to data management and transformation.

This chapter covers essential core data concepts, storing data, workloads, and key roles in data management, giving you a good foundational understanding as you embark on a journey with Azure data services.

CHAPTER 2   UNDERSTANDING CORE DATA CONCEPTS

Introduction to Data Representation

Overview

The amount of data generated by devices, applications, and systems has exploded over the last few decades. We have data all around us and in various forms and structures. In times of large, up-to-date amounts of data processing, this is where artificial intelligence becomes sophisticated.

Different data tokens are the internal way we represent data for storing and processing. Working with different types of data like structured, semi-structured, and unstructured is a common problem faced across different industries, and data professionals must learn how to work with each of them. Data analysis helps generate valuable insights that serve as the basis for significant business decisions.

All companies worldwide should possess the power to gather, record, and process data. In this chapter, you will learn how to work with common data workloads and multiple ways to store and express your data. This module will lay the groundwork for you to learn about data processing methods and services.

Ways to Represent Data

- Structured data
- Semi-structured data
- Unstructured data

Figure 2-1 illustrates the representation of structured, semi-structured, and unstructured data.

CHAPTER 2　UNDERSTANDING CORE DATA CONCEPTS

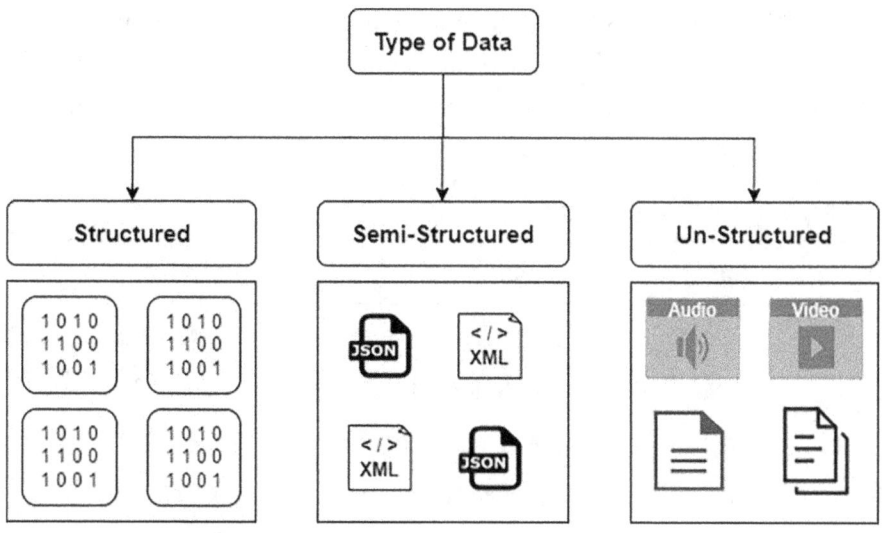

Figure 2-1. *Type of Data*

Structured Data

Structured data is a highly organized type of data. It refers to data that has a defined schema and is stored in tables. This architecture, typically structured in rows and columns, contains unique records or data entries for every row and a specific kind of data residing in its column (such as a customer's name, product price, or order date). Conventional database management systems (DBMS), such as SQL-based systems, can process structured data quickly because it is highly organized and easily searchable and queryable.

It is also better for analysis because structured data adheres to strict rules or schemas and is stored in relational databases. This makes structured data very predictable and also easy to understand, which in turn allows humans to interact with it using familiar tools such as SQL queries.

Table 2-1 contains structured data about individual customers, including their unique ID, name, email address, and phone number. This table serves as a reference for managing customer-related information in a systematic and organized format.

Table 2-1. Customer Table

ID	Name	Email	Phone
1	Kumar	kumar@ntech.com	1234567890
2	David	david@tek.com	9876543210
3	Priya	Priya@ntech.com	9876123123
4	Ram	Ram@tek.com	9988776653
5	John	John@ntech.com	9000011111

Examples

- **Customer Database**: A retail business can store information about a customer such as their name, email, phone number, shipping address, and past purchases in a database. In the table, each client would generate a row, and one of these particular properties would occupy each column. This can be used to easily fetch data about clients, update them, and analyze them.

- **Inventory Management System**: An inventory database might contain organized data on items, such as their amounts, prices, suppliers, and storage places, which is relevant in manufacturing or retail. Each product is represented as a record, and product information (like product ID, name, price, and quantity in stock) is stored as columns in the database.

- **Logistics Company**: An example of structured data would be a logistics organization that could store their shipping details in an orderly manner with each shipment containing attributes like ShipmentID, Origin, Destination, ShipmentDate, DeliveryDate, Carrier, Status, and TrackingNumber. The standardization of this data helps ensure it is easily retrievable for report generation, inventory management, shipment tracking, etc.

Use Cases

- **Analytics and Reporting**: Structured data is preferred during data analysis and report generation. A business analyst might query a customer database to put together a report on sales by region or customer demographics. Its uniform and clear format ensures systematic analysis of structured data.

- **Data Consistency and Integrity**: The use of its structured format ensures data consistency and integrity by enforcing rules and relationships between data. Foreign Keys: You can use foreign keys to establish a clear relationship between customers and their orders, ensuring data accuracy and integrity.

- **Transactional Systems**: Many transactional systems rely on structured data to process orders, payments, or personnel records, for instance. This helps these systems process and store data correctly and without errors.

Real-Time Example

For example, consider a sales team's customer relationship management (CRM) system. Sales interactions, contact details, and the status of an account are some of the structured data on clients that this system maintains in a database. This data can be simply queried to help discussion staff review past conversations, monitor client involvement, and identify new sales potential. SQL queries can be used to quickly pull up reports that show sales numbers, sales trends, customer demographics, etc.

Semi-structured Data

Semi-structured data, which cannot be easily framed into the confines of the structured data, is nonetheless somewhat organized. Markers or tags are often used to separate other elements in semi-structured data, to make the data more readable when compared to structured data, which remains in the form of tables with predefined columns and rows. These files are most commonly found using JSON, XML, and YAML (YAML Ain't Markup Language) format.

While semi-structured data does not have the rigid schema of structured data, it still contains enough organizational features (such as tags, key-value pairs, or nested structures) to make it useful for processing and analysis. Semi-structured data provides a level of flexibility in how the information is stored, enabling an easy representation of complex, dynamic, or diverse data sources.

Examples

- **JSON Data:** JSON is used to send data between the web application and the server. For example, product data may have attributes such as ProductID,

ProductName, Price, and Category and may be stored on an ecommerce platform in a JSON format. Unlike structured data, the structure is flexible because, depending on the fed category, some products may have additional features (size or color, for instance).

Example of JSON data:

```
{
    "ProductID": "12345",
    "ProductName": "Laptop",
    "Price": 799.99,
    "Category": "Electronics",
    "Attributes": {
        "Brand": "Dell",
        "Size": "15 inches",
        "Color": "Black"
    }
}
```

- **XML Data**: XML is often used for transferring data in many industries. For example, the XML format for a book catalog might have elements for Title, Author, Publisher, and ISBN. As different books may have different metadata such as PageCount or Genre, the structure is more flexible than standard relational databases.

  Example of XML data:

  ```
  <Book>
    <Title>Azure Data Fundamentals Companion</Title>
    <Author>Naveen Kumar M</Author>
    <Publisher>Apress</Publisher>
  ```

```
    979-8-8688-1683-30987654321</ISBN>
    <Attributes>
      <PageCount>180</PageCount>
      <Genre>Technology</Genre>
    </Attributes>
  </Book>
```

Use Cases

- **Web Services and APIs**: Many web services and APIs exchange data using semi-structured data types (e.g., XML or JSON). An example of this would be a service from a weather provider similar to the one I defined above, where the result might be JSON containing current temperature, windspeed, and forecast for a region.

- **Logs and Events**: System logs, event tracking, and sensor data are all examples of semi-structured data. Each log entry or event may contain a different set of attributes depending on the type of data source. This flexibility allows for rapid adaptation to changing data sources.

- **Data Interchange**: Semi-structured data is ideal for sharing information between two systems that do not have a similar schema. A retailer and a supplier may, for example, exchange product information in a semi-structured way to aid in inventory management.

CHAPTER 2   UNDERSTANDING CORE DATA CONCEPTS

Real-Time Example

Consider a social networking website like Twitter. The other difficulty in storing information in a constant schema is the fact that the attributes of a tweet, for example, timestamp, user mentions, hashtags, etc., may vary from tweet to tweet. Using the JSON language, the software is able to use flexible fields to store this data since individual tweets have different structures. For example, some tweets may have additional media (images or videos), whereas other tweets do not. Due to its flexibility, semi-structured data is well suited for representing flexible content, such as social media postings.

Unstructured Data

Unstructured data is information that does not have a predefined data model or is not organized in a predefined manner. It can take the form of text documents but also photos, movies, audio files, or social media posts. Unlike structured or semi-structured data, unstructured data does not follow any rules or model. Nevertheless, unstructured data often has valuable insight embedded, which can be processed and analyzed given the right tools.

The challenge with unstructured data is that to extract value from it, you need advanced techniques like machine learning, computer vision, or natural language processing (NLP). Unstructured data is often stored in data lakes or file systems that support different file formats.

Examples

- **Text Documents:** A collection of text documents, including emails, reports, or blog posts, is a type of unstructured data. Even though these files contain valuable information, they are not organized like structured data; therefore, analysis becomes more difficult.

CHAPTER 2   UNDERSTANDING CORE DATA CONCEPTS

- **Pictures and Videos**: Images and videos can be considered as two popular types of unstructured data. For example, a healthcare organization needs to retain medical images (such as MRIs or X-rays) and needs machine learning algorithms to see if there are any trends or abnormalities.

- **Audio Files**: Audio data is another category of unstructured data, consisting of voice messages, podcasts, and customer support call recordings. Audio data can be transcribed through speech-to-text algorithms, helping to assess content.

Use Cases

- **Sentiment Analysis**: Businesses can find out whether the consumer feedback (social media, emails, reviews, etc.) is positive, negative, or neutral. This type of analysis is most effective when applied to unstructured data, like written documents and social media posts.

- **Image Recognition and Classification**: In sectors such as security and healthcare, unstructured picture data is processed to either identify patterns in or classify objects. AI can be applied, for example, to recognize faces in video footage of people under surveillance or to analyze medical imaging for signs of disease.

- **Voice Recognition and Speech-to-Text**: Audio data that is unstructured can be transcribed and analyzed to learn things about the client. As another example, a customer support center may review recorded phone calls to identify common problems among clients or to measure satisfaction of customers.

Real-Time Example

For example, take the case of a logistics company analyzing customer support call recordings. These audio files fall into the unstructured data category since they do not have a given structure. It uses speech-to-text technology to transcribe the calls and natural language processing to analyze the content, identifying common issues or customer sentiment, to help them improve service quality and resolve recurring problems.

Data Storage Options

In this module, you will gain the skills to select the correct file format and store data appropriately to ensure efficacy and efficiency while working on data on Azure or any other cloud platform. You've learned about the basics of every computer system and file storage. While files can be stored on USB devices, external drives, or personal PCs, the scope and safety of these alternatives are limited.

When it comes to companies, though, they tend to utilize shared file storage systems, which are often cloud based, to store their key data in a central location. Cloud-based storage solutions offer several advantages, including scalability to manage increasing data volumes, enhanced security to protect sensitive information, and cost efficiency as they eliminate the need for large on-premises hardware. Cloud storage can use these advantages to write jobs of big datasets while non-stop keeping availability and flexibility.

There are several aspects to consider: the file format to choose.

- The type of data (structured, semi-structured, or unstructured)
- Whether the applications and services that need access to the data are compatible
- If the files should be human-readable or efficient for storage and as a processing format

Here are a few common and optimized formats for file storage.

Delimited Text Files

Delimited text files are simple text files that contain data in rows and columns. In addition, rows are split by a new line character (\n), and columns are split by a delimiter (some character). Because of their simplicity, portability, and ability to be parsed with most computer languages and tools, these files are widely used for interchange and transmission of data between different systems.

Key Characteristics

1. **Delimiter**: Set of characters which maintains fields (columns) under a row. Common delimiters include
    - Comma (,) – CSV (Comma-Separated Values)
    - Tab (\t) – TSV (Tab-Separated Values)
    - Pipe (|) – Pipe-Separated Files
    - Semicolon (;) – Often used in European data formats

CHAPTER 2   UNDERSTANDING CORE DATA CONCEPTS

2. **Row Separation**: Each row of data is represented as a new line in the file.

3. **Plain Text**: Human-readable and editable using text editors.

4. **File Extensions**: Common extensions include .csv, .tsv, and .txt.

Example
CSV File Example

Filename: employees.csv

> EmployeeID,FirstName,LastName,Department,Salary
>
> 101,Prem,Kumar,Engineering,75000
>
> 102,David,William,Marketing,68000
>
> 103,Bob,Brown,Sales,72000

TSV File Example

Filename: products.tsv

ProductID	ProductName	Category	Price
1	Keyboard	Electronics	29.99
2	Mouse	Electronics	19.99
3	Notebook	Stationery	5.49

CHAPTER 2 UNDERSTANDING CORE DATA CONCEPTS

Pipe-Separated File Example

Filename: orders.txt

OrderID|CustomerName|OrderDate|TotalAmount

2001|Alice Johnson|2025-01-01|150.50

2002|David Miller|2025-01-02|300.00

JavaScript Object Notation (JSON)

JavaScript Object Notation (JSON) is a lightweight data-interchange format that is easy for humans to read and write and easy for machines to parse and generate. It can be utilized in nearly all programming languages, but its primary purpose for web applications is for sharing data between a server and a client.

Key Characteristics

- **Lightweight**: Slim and short, making it perfect for sending data over networks.
- **Human-Readable**: The format is human-readable and easy to understand.
- **Self-Descriptive**: Data is organized in a key-value structure that describes itself.
- **Language-Agnostic**: There is a parser for JSON in almost every programming language out there.

CHAPTER 2   UNDERSTANDING CORE DATA CONCEPTS

JSON Structure

JSON data structure has two main types that enable you to represent data:

1. **Objects**: Ranges of key-value pairs wrapped in { }.

   - Keys must be strings, and values can be strings, numbers, booleans, arrays, objects, or null.

   Example:

   ```
   {
      "name": "John Doe",
      "age": 30,
      "isMarried": false
   }
   ```

2. **Arrays**: An ordered list of comma-separated values within square brackets [].

   Example:

   ```
   ["apple", "banana", "cherry"]
   ```

Example JSON Data

For example, the following is JSON data that represents a user profile:

```
{
  "user": {
    "id": 101,
    "name": "Alice Johnson",
    "email": "alice@example.com",
    "isVerified": true,
    "roles": ["admin", "editor"],
    "profile": {
      "age": 28,
```

```
      "city": "New York",
      "preferences": {
        "theme": "dark",
        "language": "en"
      }
    }
  }
}
```

Extensible Markup Language (XML)

Extensible Markup Language (XML) is a markup language designed to store and exchange data in a human-readable and machine-readable format as well as in a structured and platform-independent way. Its human- and machine-readable format allows for flexible data interchange across many systems.

The standard XML defined by W3C allows us to create custom tags, properties, and formats for representing data. XML is primarily concerned with describing and transporting data, whereas HTML is focused on dictating the presentation of data.

Key Characteristics

1. **Self-Descriptive Structure**: XML is self-descriptive, which makes it easy to understand.

2. **Platform Independent**: XML can be used on different platforms and programming languages.

3. **Extensibility**: You can read more about the exact format of the data you can send to the parser. As I mentioned on the first point, users can extend the basic tags to add custom tags to fulfill their needs.

CHAPTER 2   UNDERSTANDING CORE DATA CONCEPTS

4. **Hierarchical Structure**: The XML model organizes data in a hierarchical format, including parent and child relationships.

5. **Unicode Support**: XML has support for many languages and character sets.

6. **Validation**: The XML documents can be validated using a **Document Type Definition (DTD)** or **XML Schema Definition (XSD)** to confirm correctness.

Example:

```xml
<?xml version="1.0" encoding="UTF-8"?>
<library>
    <book id="1">
        <title>Learning XML</title>
        <Author>John Doe</author>
        <publisher>Tech Press</publisher>
        <price>29.99</price>
    </book>
    <book id="2">
        <title>Mastering XML</title>
        <Author>Jane Smith</author>
        <publisher>CodeWorld</publisher>
        <price>39.99</price>
    </book>
</library>
```

Binary Large Object (BLOB)

A BLOB is a collection of binary data stored as a single entity in a database or file system. BLOBs are commonly used to store multimedia objects such as images, videos, audio, and other similar data. Typically, the database sees them as opaque data; in other words, it stores the BLOB without decoding its contents.

BLOBs can be used to save large binary files or serialized objects that do not align well with traditional relational database tables. They allow applications to efficiently access and store data without needing to translate it to and from text or other formats.

Characteristics of a BLOB

1. **Binary Data**: A BLOB can be thought of as a binary large object, which is data not in a fixed format but in the form of a data stream.

2. **Large Size**: BLOBs are used to store a big size of data, i.e., megabytes to gigabytes.

3. **Database Support**: Most relational databases like SQL Server, MySQL, PostgreSQL, and Oracle have BLOB as a data type.

4. **Non-Human-Readable**: BLOBs are not human-readable as they store data in binary format.

5. **Flexible Use**: Supports different file types – images (JPEG, PNG), documents (PDF, DOCX), videos (MP4).

Example:

- **Images**: Formats like JPEG, PNG, BMP, TIFF, and GIF store image data as binary.
- **Audio**: Formats like MP3, WAV, AAC, FLAC, and OGG store audio data as binary.
- **Video**: Formats such as MP4, AVI, MKV, MOV, and WMV store video and multimedia data as binary.
- **Documents**: Formats like PDF, DOC, DOCX, XLS, and XLSX.

Optimized File Formats

Optimized file formats are specifically designed to store data in a way that optimizes processing, query performance, and storage efficiency. These formats are necessary for the handling and processing of big data. A few popular optimized file formats are Avro, ORC, and Parquet; each has special features that make it suitable for specific scenarios.

Avro

Apache Avro is a data serialization system developed to provide a compact, schema-based mechanism for data persistence and transport. It describes the structure of data using a schema, so serialization and deserialization are consistent across various systems. Avro files are self-describing and easy to interpret since the schema is encapsulated in a file and saved in JSON format without any extra metadata.

Avro supports a more efficient and compact format when compared to text-based file formats like XML or JSON, as it encodes the data in binary format. Moreover, the format enables schema evolution (e.g., adding new fields or modifying optional items) without breaking compatibility with existing data. Its adaptability makes Avro ideal for large data applications in which data schemas evolve over time.

ORC (Optimized Row Columnar)

Optimized Row Columnar (ORC) is a highly efficient columnar storage format optimized for big data processing in the distributed Hadoop ecosystem such as Apache Hive. This way, it stores the data in columns rather than rows, making it super efficient for compressing the large amount of data and answering queries faster as it needs to retrieve only the columns relevant for the query. ORC has integrated metadata with its file, such as row counts, data types, and min/max values, which means systems can skip searching those sections of the data, allowing for better query performance.

ORC provides support for highly efficient compression techniques, such as run-length encoding and dictionary encoding, per column based on the data type, which reduces the amount of storage space required by the format. Its splittable format allows distributed propositions over multiple nodes in distributed environments, so it's very well suited for large-scale data analytics. ORC is popular in big data ecosystems because of its storage efficiency, query optimization, and scalability.

Parquet

Parquet is a column-oriented storage format that has been designed for analytics workflows with large-scale data processing in distributed systems like Apache Hadoop, Apache Spark, or Apache Hive. It reduces I/O operations and speeds up processing by organizing data by columns as opposed to rows, enabling queries to read just the required columns. This columnar approach also allows for better file compression since you can pack similar types of data into a column rather than grouping them by row with differing data types.

Are you familiar with the Parquet format? It stores metadata, like min/max values and statistics for each column, which can be used at query time for efficient filtering and predictive pushdown. Parquet is widely used for data storage and retrieval due to its performance, efficiency, and support for structured and semi-structured data.

Explore Databases

Databases are structured information sets that allow efficient management, retrieval, and storage of information. They power everything from simple websites to complex enterprise applications and are critical to modern applications. There are many types of databases, and they can be categorized broadly as relational and non-relational (or NoSQL) databases. Every one of these forms of databases is created to meet unique needs in terms of storing and using data.

Relational Databases

There are relational databases which use structured tables with rows and columns to store data. Each table represents an entity like customers or items, and keys (primary and foreign keys) are used to create relationships between the tables as shown in Figure 2-2. This is a widely used method, ensuring data consistency, integrity, and the ability to access data through Structured Query Language (SQL).

Examples of Relational Databases

1. Microsoft SQL Server
2. MySQL
3. PostgreSQL
4. Oracle Database
5. SQLite

CHAPTER 2   UNDERSTANDING CORE DATA CONCEPTS

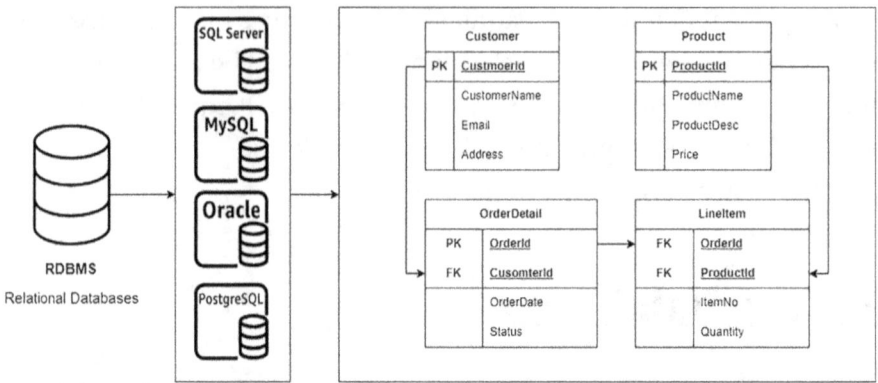

Figure 2-2. *Relational Databases*

Non-relational Databases

NoSQL provides support for unstructured, semi-structured, or rapidly changing data. Since they do not depend on predefined schemas, they are more flexible and scalable for some use cases.

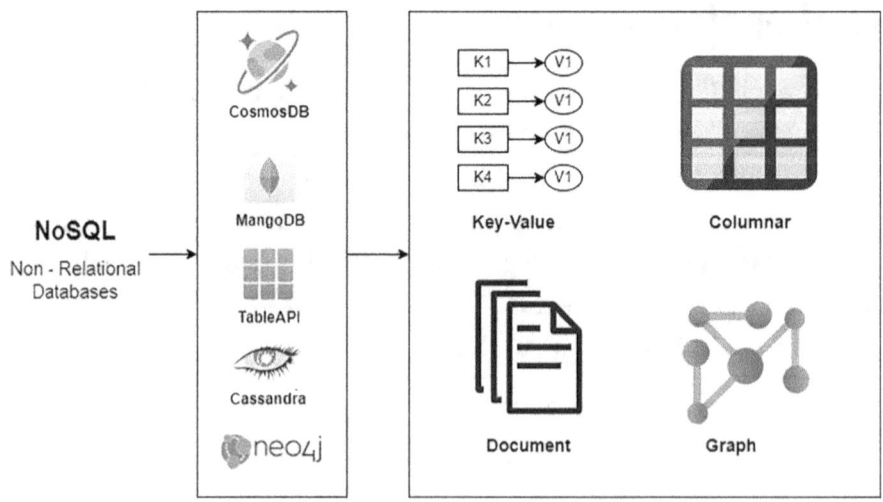

Figure 2-3. *Non-relational Databases*

CHAPTER 2   UNDERSTANDING CORE DATA CONCEPTS

These are the four most common types of non-relational databases as illustrated in Figure 2-3:

1. **Key-Value Databases**: These are used to store data as a collection of key-value pairs, where KEY is a unique identifier of an associated value.

   Examples: Redis, DynamoDB

2. **Document Databases**: Store data in document formats (JSON or BSON) to allow representation of complex data structures.

   Examples: MongoDB, CouchDB

3. **Column-Family Databases:** Organizing data in column families instead of rows, like column stores, saves space and allows for efficient storage and retrieval of analytical queries.

   Examples: Apache Cassandra, HBase

4. **Graph Databases**: Designed around relationships, they use nodes for entities and edges for their connections.

   Examples: Neo4j, Amazon Neptune

Data Workloads

Data workloads refer to all the various ways that businesses collect, store, processes, and analyzes data to support decision-making, company operations, and strategy. There are workloads based on the type of data you have and how you want to use it, like real-time transactions, analytical reporting, or long-term storage and retrieval.

The common types of data workloads:

- Online Transaction Processing (OLTP)
- Online Analytical Processing (OLAP)
- Data Warehousing

Transactional Workloads
Online Transaction Processing (OLTP)

OLTP stands for Online Transaction Processing. This describes a type of data processing system designed for real-time handling and support of database transactional data. OLTP systems are designed to process many small online transactions, typically with small amounts of data (insert, update, delete, query).

Key Characteristics of OLTP Systems

1. **High Transaction Volume**: Process transactions, for example, online purchases and bank transfers, at tens of thousands per second.

2. **Real-Time Processing**: Transactions are processed immediately as they occur.

3. **Data Integrity**: Guarantees consistency and accuracy of data using concepts like constraints, indexes, and relational models.

4. **Concurrency**: Allows multiple users to access and modify the database concurrently with no or minimal performance degradation.

5. **Fast Query Execution**: OLTP systems are optimized for fast reads and writes, typically out of small datasets.

6. **Normalization**: Database schemas have a very high normalization for OLTP systems as they try to eliminate the redundancy of data.

ACID Properties of OLTP

OLTP systems follow the ACID properties to maintain the integrity and consistency of the data:

1. **Atomicity**: Ensures that all parts of a transaction are completed successfully. If any part fails, the entire transaction is rolled back.

   Example: Transferring funds between accounts either completes fully or does not happen at all.

2. **Consistency**: Guarantees that a transaction transitions the database from one valid state to another, maintaining all defined rules and constraints.

   Example: A balance update in a banking system ensures the total funds remain accurate.

3. **Isolation**: Ensures that concurrent transactions do not interfere with each other, providing consistent results.

   Example: Two users withdrawing funds simultaneously will not affect each other's transactions.

CHAPTER 2   UNDERSTANDING CORE DATA CONCEPTS

4. **Durability**: Ensures that once a transaction is committed, the changes are permanent, even in case of a system crash.

    Example: Once a payment is processed, it remains recorded even if the system restarts.

The following are the Azure OLTP services as given in Figure 2-4:

- Azure SQL Database
- SQL Server in Virtual Machine
- Azure Database for MySQL
- Azure Database for PostgreSQL

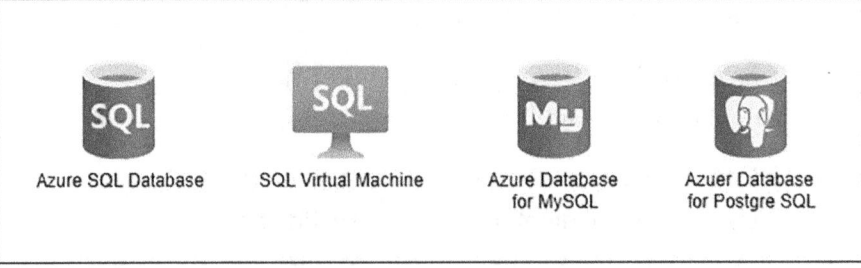

Figure 2-4. Azure OLTP Services

Analytical Workloads
Online Analytical Processing (OLAP)

Analytical data processing often utilizes read-only (or read-mostly) systems that store vast amounts of historical data or business indicators. This data, at a moment in time or a sequence of snapshots, can form the basis for analytics. OLAP systems are developed to process

CHAPTER 2 UNDERSTANDING CORE DATA CONCEPTS

multidimensional data and handle complex analytical queries, often over aggregated data. These tools help the user to generate business intelligence and to apply advanced analytics to large datasets.

Key Characteristics of OLAP

1. **Multidimensional Data**: In Mater Data Management (MDM), the data is arranged in a cube-like structure where each dimension is a different data insight (time, region, product, etc.), giving the ability to efficiently query data using multiple dimensions.

2. **Slice and Dice**: Users can "slice" the data (view from usefulness perspective from specific subset) and "dice" it (from different positions according to different angles).

3. **Drill Down/Up**: Users are able to drill down into the data for more granular details (e.g., from yearly to monthly data) and drill up for more aggregated views.

4. **Pivoting**: It helps you reorganize the data so that you can see it from different angles.

5. **Real-Time Querying**: OLAP is ideal for extensive data, as it allows for rapid querying of premises.

The following are the Azure OLAP services as given in Figure 2-5:

- SQL Server with Column Store index
- Azure Analysis Service
- Azure Synapse Analytics
- Azure SQL Data Warehouse

CHAPTER 2   UNDERSTANDING CORE DATA CONCEPTS

- Azure Cosmos DB (with Analytical Store)
- Power BI (with Azure Integration)

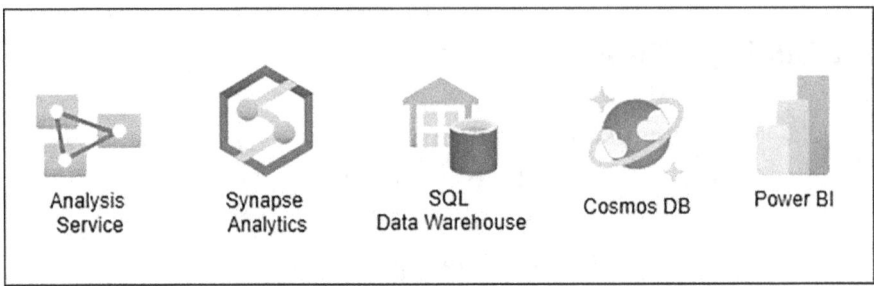

Figure 2-5. Azure OLAP Services

Data Warehouse

What is a data warehouse? A data warehouse is a central data repository for reporting and analyzing data. It serves as a foundation for supporting BI and reporting tools and analytical activities. It combines data from data warehouses, transactional systems, databases, and computer systems into a single format that is optimized for reporting and querying and not transaction processing.

Key Characteristics of a Data Warehouse

1. **Subject Oriented**: Types of data can be organized around various business dimensions (like sales, inventory, finance).

2. **Integrated**: Merged data from various sources with consistency in naming convention, formats, and encoding.

CHAPTER 2   UNDERSTANDING CORE DATA CONCEPTS

3. **Time Variant**: Keeps the historical data to enable the evolution over their duration and timestamp in order to provide the details of the changes occurring.

4. **Non-volatile**: The data stores in the data warehouse when all data has been written to its final state.

Components of a Data Warehouse

1. **Data Sources**: The data comes from systems, operational databases, flat files, or external sources.

2. **ETL (Extract, Transform, Load)**: A process that extracts data from sources, transforms it into the right format, and loads it into the data warehouse.

3. **Data Storage**: This is the database or storage layer where the transformed data is stored, typically in the star or snowflake schema.

4. **OLAP Cubes**: Multidimensional data structures designed to allow for fast retrieval of data by analysis tools to allow for multidimensional analysis, enabling users to view data from a variety of perspectives.

5. **BI Tools**: Using tools (e.g., Tableau, Power BI, etc.) for users to visualize and analyze data.

CHAPTER 2   UNDERSTANDING CORE DATA CONCEPTS

Key Differences Between Transactional and Analytical Workloads

The key differences between OLTP (Online Transaction Processing) and OLAP (Online Analytical Processing) are shown in Table 2-2.

Table 2-2. *OLTP and OLAP Features*

Feature	OLTP	OLAP
Purpose	Designed for managing day-to-day transactional data, typically used for operational tasks such as order processing, inventory management, and customer data	Designed for complex querying and analysis of historical data, supporting decision-making and strategic planning, typically used for business intelligence and reporting
Data Structure	Data is stored in normalized relational databases to reduce redundancy and ensure consistency, typically with many tables	Data is stored in multidimensional models (e.g., star schema or snowflake schema), often denormalized for fast querying
Transactions	Supports a high volume of small transactions, such as INSERT, UPDATE, and DELETE, with each transaction affecting a few rows	Supports fewer, larger queries, usually involving aggregations over vast amounts of data
Query Complexity	Queries are generally simple and involve operations like searching, inserting, or updating records	Queries are more complex and often involve aggregations, groupings, and calculations over large datasets

(*continued*)

CHAPTER 2   UNDERSTANDING CORE DATA CONCEPTS

Table 2-2. (*continued*)

Feature	OLTP	OLAP
Performance	Prioritizes fast processing of transactional operations and ensures data integrity, usually requiring high throughput and low latency	Prioritizes fast querying and reporting, with performance optimized for complex analytical queries on large datasets
Data Volume	Typically handles smaller datasets, as the data volume is focused on day-to-day operations	Handles large datasets, often from multiple years, used for in-depth analysis and reporting
Users	Primarily used by front-end applications, transactional systems, and operational staff (e.g., cashiers, salespeople)	Used by analysts, managers, and decision-makers who need to perform in-depth data analysis and reporting
Update Frequency	Data is updated frequently, with real-time updates for transactions	Data is typically updated in batches or through ETL processes, with updates occurring periodically

Roles and Responsibilities in Data Workloads

Data Workload Roles: There are different roles involved in managing, processing, and interpreting data in context of workload.

Here's an overview of the key roles and their responsibilities.

CHAPTER 2   UNDERSTANDING CORE DATA CONCEPTS

1. Database Administrator (DBA)

The DBA (Database Administrator) is responsible for the management, security, and performance of databases. They guarantee databases are accessible, optimized, and secure.

Key Responsibilities

- **Database Maintenance**: Regularly monitor and optimize database performance, ensuring that databases run smoothly and are efficient.

- **Backup and Recovery**: Implement robust backup and recovery strategies to ensure data integrity and availability in case of failures.

- **Security**: Enforce database security policies, including setting up user roles and permissions to prevent unauthorized access.

- **Data Integrity**: Ensure data consistency and accuracy, handling data corruption issues when they arise.

- **Migration and Upgrades**: Manage database upgrades, migrations, and patching to ensure systems are up to date.

- **Query Optimization**: Help with the optimization of queries to improve performance, especially for complex transactions.

2. Data Engineer

A Data Engineer develops and maintains systems and infrastructure that enable the collection, storage, and transformation of vast amounts of data. They can also be seen as working on data pipelines and working closely with data scientists and analysts.

CHAPTER 2   UNDERSTANDING CORE DATA CONCEPTS

Key Responsibilities

- **Data Pipeline Development**: Build and maintain scalable data pipelines to ingest, process, and store data from various sources (e.g., databases, APIs, logs).

- **ETL (Extract, Transform, Load)**: Implement ETL processes to clean, transform, and load data into data warehouses, data lakes, or databases.

- **Data Modeling**: Design data models to ensure efficient storage and retrieval. This may involve normalizing or denormalizing data and setting up indexing strategies.

- **Automation**: Automate data flows and processes to handle repetitive tasks and ensure timely data availability.

- **Performance Optimization**: Ensure that data systems are scalable and optimized for performance, especially when dealing with large datasets.

- **Collaboration with Data Scientists**: Work closely with data scientists to ensure that the data infrastructure supports advanced analytics and machine learning tasks.

3. Data Analyst

The role of a Data Analyst is to interpret data, thereby assisting organizations in making informed decisions. They are used to data that is already modeled and cleanly mapped in databases or data marts.

Key Responsibilities

- **Data Analysis**: Analyze datasets to identify trends, patterns, and insights that can inform business strategies.

- **Reporting and Visualization**: Develop reports and dashboards using tools like Power BI, Tableau, or Excel to present findings in an understandable and actionable format.

- **Business Intelligence**: Work with stakeholders to understand their data needs and ensure that the reports and insights provided align with business objectives.

- **Data Validation**: Verify data integrity to ensure that the data used for analysis is accurate and reliable.

- **Collaboration**: Work closely with both data engineers (to access the data) and business teams (to understand the requirements and communicate insights).

Explore Data Services

Data Services in Azure

One of their major assets is the Azure platform, which includes a huge selection of services for the management, storage, and analysis of data across multiple applications. These services enable organizations to address various data storage, management, and analytics requirements while ensuring scalability, performance, and security. These services make it easier to work with both structured and unstructured data, engage

CHAPTER 2   UNDERSTANDING CORE DATA CONCEPTS

with machine learning and artificial intelligence, and perform large-scale analytics. They are designed to serve different user types (data engineer, analyst, or DBAs).

1. Azure SQL

This service is referred to as Azure SQL and is built for on-premises or cloud-based SQL Server workloads and provides managed database services with varying deployment models to meet unique needs:

- **Azure SQL Database**: A fully managed relational database offering in the cloud for cloud applications. It offers built-in intelligence for performance tuning with high availability, scalability, and security.

- **Azure SQL Managed Instance**: A service that provides a fully managed instance of SQL Server in the cloud with near-complete compatibility with SQL Server for customers. It enables support for broader SQL Server workloads like SQL Agent and cross-db queries.

- **Azure SQL VM**: A VM running on SQL Server with full control over the server and database configuration. It is ideal for customers looking to lift and shift existing SQL Server workloads to Azure with little change.

2. Open Source Databases in Azure

Azure supports popular open source relational databases, offering fully managed services for developers who prefer open source technologies:

- **Azure Database for MySQL**: A fully managed MySQL database service that provides built-in high availability, automated backups, and scaling

- **Azure Database for MariaDB**: A fully managed MariaDB database service suitable for customers who are using the MariaDB community version

- **Azure Database for PostgreSQL**: A fully managed PostgreSQL database service with features such as automatic scaling, high availability, and data encryption

3. Azure Cosmos DB

Azure Cosmos DB is a mission-critical, globally distributed, multi-model database service. It supports key-value, document, graph, and column-family data models. Indeed, it is optimal for applications with high availability and multi-region responsiveness due to low latency and elastic scalability.

4. Azure Storage

Azure Storage provides scalable and durable cloud storage solutions for unstructured data:

- **Blob Containers**: For storing large amounts of unstructured data like images, videos, or documents.

- **File Shares**: An Azure file share is a cloud-based file system that can be accessed using the SMB (Server Message Block) or NFS (Network File System) protocol.

- **Tables**: Azure Table Storage is a NoSQL key-value store for storing large amounts of structured data.

CHAPTER 2   UNDERSTANDING CORE DATA CONCEPTS

5. Azure Data Factory

Azure Data Factory is a cloud-based data integration service that allows you to orchestrate and automate data workflows. It facilitates data movement, transformation, and loading (ETL/ELT) across various sources, including on-premises and cloud storage.

6. Microsoft Fabric

Microsoft Fabric is a unified data platform that combines data engineering, data science, data warehousing, and business intelligence. Fabric supports

- Data Engineering
- Data Science
- Data Lakehouse
- Data Warehousing
- Real-Time Analytics
- BI (Business Intelligence) with Power BI Integration
- Azure Synapse Analytics

It allows organizations to simplify data management and integrate various data processes.

7. Azure Databricks

Azure Databricks is a cloud-native analytics platform based on Apache Spark. It enables data engineering, data science, and machine learning workloads. Databricks allows other users on the data and tableau side to seamlessly work together to explore the data, prepare the data, and run advanced analytics with Spark-based processing capabilities built in.

8. Azure Stream Analytics

Azure Stream Analytics is a real-time data stream processing service. It is suitable for processing real-time analytics and monitoring streaming data coming from devices, sensors, social media, and other sources.

9. Azure Data Explorer

Azure Data Explorer is a fast and highly scalable data exploration service to analyze large volumes of data. It is tailored for high-frequency log and telemetry data and leverages low-latency query processing for interactive exploration of large datasets.

10. Microsoft Purview

We only have Microsoft Purview as a unified data governance solution that makes it easy to manage and govern cloud and on-premises data schemes across Azure, other cloud platforms, or your on-premises platforms. It offers functionality such as data cataloging, data lineage, compliance tracking, and data classification.

Roles and Services

The roles which interact with Azure data services are Data Engineers, Data Analysts, and DBAs. Now let's get into these roles and the services they typically use:

- **Data Engineers**: Data Engineers typically work with services such as Azure Data Factory, Azure Databricks, Azure SQL, and Microsoft Fabric for data pipeline engineering, data preparation, and data infrastructure management.

- **Data Analysts**: Use Azure SQL, Azure Databricks, Azure Stream Analytics, and Microsoft Fabric for running queries on data, analyzing data, and generating reports. They are often heavily dependent on Azure Synapse and Power BI for visualization and insights of the data.

- **DBAs**: When we talk about database administrators, we are referring to those who manage database instances such as Azure SQL Database, Azure SQL Managed Instance, Azure SQL VM, and open source databases (like MySQL, MariaDB, and PostgreSQL). They are responsible for securing and performing those database instances with high availability.

Summary

This chapter introduced readers to the basic principles of data representation, storage, and management, which form the foundation for understanding how data is organized, processed, and used in contemporary systems. Here's a summary of what we covered:

Types of Data

- **Structured Data**: Data that is highly organized and follows a well-defined schema, generally stored in the form of tables with rows and columns, and used a lot in transactional systems and analytics (like RDBMS)

- **Semi-structured Data**: Data that has a certain degree of organization but does not conform to a rigid structure, commonly seen in formats such as JSON or XML, which is widely used in web services, APIs, and log files

CHAPTER 2   UNDERSTANDING CORE DATA CONCEPTS

- **Unstructured Data**: Data with no predetermined structure, including text documents, photos, and videos, requiring sophisticated tools (like machine learning) to process

Data Storage Options

- In this section, we talked about data storage formats, delimited text file (CSV, TSV), JSON, XML, and optimized storage techniques like Avro, ORC, and Parquet which are used for efficiently storing and processing large datasets.

- Cloud-based storage solutions are a necessity for modern data management due to their scalability, security, and cost efficiency, which are core attributes of Azure as well.

Databases

- Databases come in various types, that are broadly classified into two main categories: (1) databases for structured data – examples are SQL Server, MySQL, etc., and (2) databases for unstructured or semi-structured data (NoSQL) – examples are MongoDB, Cassandra, etc.

- From transactional systems to big data analytics, every type of database has a specific use case.

Data Workloads

We exposed two main types of data processing workloads:

- **Transactional Workloads (OLTP)**: Designed for transactional work such as order processing or banking.

- **Analytical Workloads (OLAP)**: OLAP databases are optimized for running complex queries and analyzing historical data, being used in business intelligence and reporting.

Roles in Data Management

Some key roles involved in data workloads are

- **Database Administrators (DBAs)**: Ensuring database performance, security, and upkeep

- **Data Engineers**: Designing and maintaining data pipelines and systems for processing data

- **Data Analysts**: Utilizing usage data to help generate insights or drive decisions

Azure Data Services

Azure offers a full range of data services, such as

- Managed relational databases with Azure SQL

- Azure Cosmos DB for global distributed multi-model databases

- Azure Data Factory for data integration and ETL/ELT workflows

- Azure Synapse Analytics and Azure Databricks for big data and advanced analytics processing

- Microsoft Fabric: The unified analytics platform for data engineering, science, warehousing, and business intelligence

CHAPTER 3

Working with Relational Data on Azure

To get started, this chapter covers the core principles of relational databases and how they are used in the context of Azure. You will learn the basics of relational data, how data needs to be normalized to be effectively structured, and how relational data is supported by common SQL statements and database objects.

The chapter gives an overview of the Azure SQL family, which is a family of relational database services (Azure SQL Database, Managed Instance, and Server on VMs) and their features and scenarios. It also dives into how Azure supports popular open source relational databases, such as MySQL, PostgreSQL, and MariaDB, and how they are applied in modern data solutions.

In this chapter, you will be introduced to relational data concepts and various relational database services on Azure that will help you choose and deploy the right service for your data needs.

CHAPTER 3 WORKING WITH RELATIONAL DATA ON AZURE

Relational Data Concepts
Features of Relational Data
Overview

In the early days of computing, every application used a unique way of storing data, which left us with a fragmented and inefficient landscape. Whether it meant pulling information or manipulating it, developers needed to know intimately each individual data structure, making application development clumsy and prone to error. Managing and optimizing the performance of these ad hoc storage methods proved to be cumbersome.

These issues prompted the development of the relational database model, which brought forth a standardized method for structuring and accessing data. Rather than copying in arbitrary application-specific structures, the relational model surfaces data in tables, a logical, human-intuitive, and exceedingly efficient format. This consistency also allows any application to work with data as the common interface without having detailed knowledge about the underlying storage mechanics.

The relational model uses tables to represent data relationships, offering a flexible and scalable approach to managing structured information while maintaining data integrity, minimizing redundancy, and supporting advanced querying capabilities. This was a game changer in database management, enabling a new era of modern high-performance applications.

Relational Data

Relational data is structured in a form that organizes data into multiple tables (also known as relations) of rows and columns. The relationships that define how these tables are related to each other enable efficient data storage, retrieval, and manipulation.

CHAPTER 3   WORKING WITH RELATIONAL DATA ON AZURE

Example of Relational Data

Figure 3-1 illustrates the Entity-Relationship (ER) diagram for the student enrollment system, depicting the relationships between Students, Departments, Courses, and Enrollments.

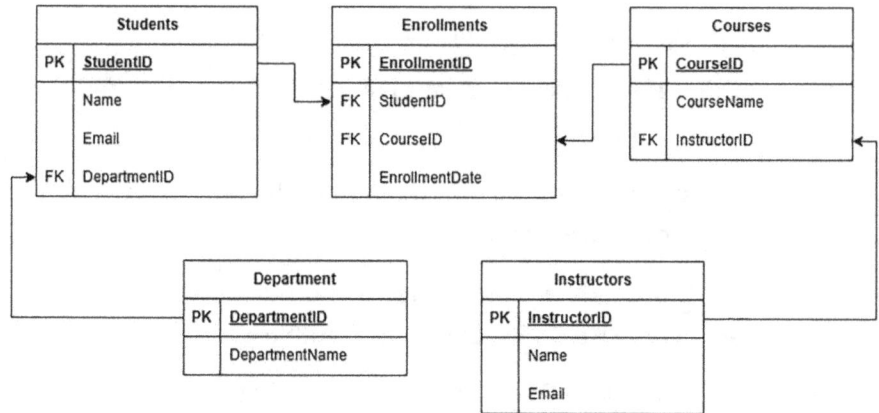

Figure 3-1. *Entity-Relationship Diagram for University Database*

Here, relationships are established using keys as illustrated in Figure 3-1:

- A **primary key** uniquely identifies a row (e.g., StudentID in the Students table).

- A **foreign key** links to a primary key in another table (e.g., DepartmentID in Students references DepartmentID in Departments).

Features of Relational Data

1. **Tables (Relations):** A structured set of data elements in rows (tuples) and columns (attributes)
2. **Primary Keys:** Distinguish each row uniquely across a table (such as StudentID)
3. **Foreign Keys:** Establish relationships between tables
4. **Normalization:** Minimizes redundancy by organizing data efficiently
5. **ACID Compliance:** Ensures transactions are Atomic, Consistent, Isolated, and Durable
6. **SQL (Structured Query Language):** Standard language for querying and managing relational data
7. **Indexes:** Improve query performance by speeding up data retrieval
8. **Constraints:** Enforce data integrity (e.g., NOT NULL, UNIQUE, CHECK)

Data Normalization

Normalization is the process that involves a series of transformation steps from one form to the next higher form. It is where large tables are broken down into smaller, relevant tables, and the data dependencies are logical.

Why Normalization?

- Reduces data redundancy (duplication of data)
- Avoids update anomalies (insertion, deletion, and modification problems)
- Improves data consistency
- Makes the database structure less complex

Levels of Normalization

Normalization consists of several progressive levels called Normal Forms (NF) where each level is a building block to the next.

1. First Normal Form (1NF)

Rules

- All values in each column have to be atomic (indivisible).
- There must be a unique row identifier (primary key).
- There will be no repeating groups or arrays in columns.

Example (Before 1NF)

OrderID	Customer	Products
1001	John David	Laptop, Mouse, Keyboard
1002	Dave Smith	Monitor, Headphones

CHAPTER 3 WORKING WITH RELATIONAL DATA ON AZURE

Problem: The "Products" column contains multiple values.

After 1NF

OrderID	Customer	Product
1001	John David	Laptop
1001	John David	Mouse
1001	John David	Keyboard
1002	Dave Smith	Monitor
1002	Dave Smith	Headphones

Problem Fixed: Each product is in a separate row.

2. Second Normal Form (2NF)

Rules

- Must be in 1NF.
- There should be no partial dependency, meaning all non-key columns should depend on the complete primary key.

Example (Before 2NF)

OrderID	ProductID	ProductName	Price
1001	P001	Laptop	50000
1001	P002	Mouse	1500
1002	P003	Monitor	5000

Problem: ProductName and Price are dependent on ProductID rather than the complete primary key, i.e., OrderID + ProductID.

CHAPTER 3 WORKING WITH RELATIONAL DATA ON AZURE

After 2NF
Orders Table

OrderID	ProductID
1001	P001
1001	P002
1002	P003

Products Table

ProductID	ProductName	Price
P001	Laptop	50000
P002	Mouse	1500
P003	Monitor	5000

Problem Fixed: It was separated into two tables to eliminate the partial dependency.

3. Third Normal Form (3NF)

Rules

- Must be in 2NF.
- There is no transitive dependency (non-key columns must depend only on key columns).

Example (Before 3NF)

StudentID	Name	DepartmentID	DepartmentName
101	Kumar	D01	Computer Science
102	Priya	D02	Mathematics

Problem: DepartmentName depends on DepartmentID, not directly on StudentID.

After 3NF
Students Table

StudentID	Name	DepartmentID
101	Kumar	D01
102	Priya	D02

Departments Table

DepartmentID	DepartmentName
D01	Computer Science
D02	Mathematics

Problem Fixed: Eliminated transitive dependency.

4. Boyce-Codd Normal Form (BCNF)

Rules

- Stricter than 3NF.
- All determinants must be superkey (a.k.a. candidate key).

Example (Before BCNF)

StudentID	Course	Professor
101	Math	Dr. Gomathi
101	Physics	Dr. Priya
102	Math	Dr. Gomathi

Problem: If a professor teaches a single course, then Professor determines Course; however, Professor is not a superkey.

After BCNF

Student Courses Table

StudentID	Course
101	Math
101	Physics
102	Math

Professor Courses Table

Professor	Course
Dr. Gomathi	Math
Dr. Priya	Physics
Dr. Gomathi	Math

Problem Fixed: Ensured all determinants are superkeys.

5. Fourth Normal Form (4NF) and Fifth Normal Form (5NF)

- **4NF**: Eliminates multi-valued dependencies
- **5NF**: Ensures lossless decomposition (no data loss when splitting tables)

When to Stop Normalizing?

- Excessive normalization can cause many joins and slow down queries.
- In some cases, we perform denormalization (i.e., we introduce redundancy) in order to obtain performance.

Databases preserve their efficiency when structured nicely using normalization. There are higher normal forms above those (BCNF, 4NF, 5NF), but most applications are designed in up to 3NF.

Explore SQL

SQL (Structured Query Language) is the standard language for managing relational databases. It allows users to

- Create and modify database structures
- Insert, update, and delete data
- Retrieve information through queries
- Control access to data

SQL is implemented in various database management systems (DBMS), each with slight variations in syntax and features.

Common RDBMS That Uses SQL

1. Microsoft SQL Server (T-SQL)

- Developed by Microsoft
- Uses Transact-SQL (T-SQL) extensions
- Tight integration with Windows ecosystem
- Features like Common Language Runtime (CLR) integration and XML support

2. MySQL

- Open source RDBMS
- Owned by Oracle
- Popular for web applications
- Known for speed and reliability

3. PostgreSQL

- Advanced open source RDBMS
- Supports complex data types (JSON, GIS)
- ACID compliant with strong standards compliance

4. MariaDB

- Fork of MySQL by original developers
- Fully open source
- Improved performance and features over MySQL

5. Oracle Database (PL/SQL)

- Enterprise-grade RDBMS
- Uses PL/SQL procedural language
- Advanced security and scalability features

SQL Command Categories

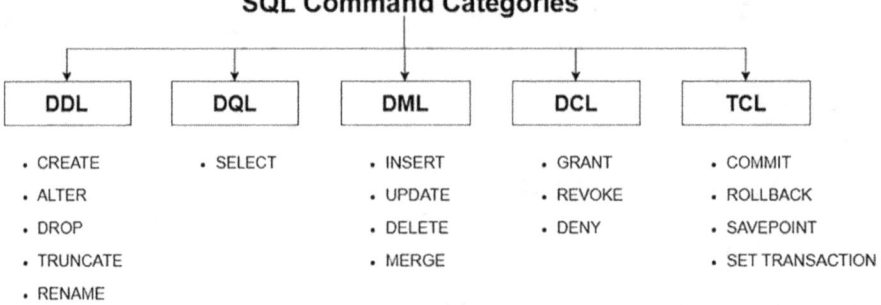

Figure 3-2. SQL Command Categories

Figure 3-2 illustrates the SQL command categories, including DDL, DQL, DML, DCL, and TCL. Each of these parts is explained in detail below.

1. DDL (Data Definition Language)

It manages database structure.
Commands

- CREATE: Creates objects
- ALTER: Modifies objects
- DROP: Deletes objects
- TRUNCATE: Removes all records
- RENAME: Renames objects

Example:

```sql
-- Create a table
CREATE TABLE Employees (
    EmployeeID INT PRIMARY KEY,
    FirstName VARCHAR(50),
    LastName VARCHAR(50),
    Department VARCHAR(50)
);

-- Alter table (add column)
ALTER TABLE Employees ADD Email VARCHAR(100);

-- Drop table
DROP TABLE Employees;

-- Truncate table (delete all data)
TRUNCATE TABLE Employees;
```

2. DQL (Data Query Language)

It retrieves data from databases.

Command

- SELECT: Retrieves data

Example:

```sql
-- Basic select
SELECT * FROM Employees;

-- Select specific columns
SELECT FirstName, LastName FROM Employees;

-- With conditions
SELECT * FROM Employees WHERE Department = 'IT';
```

CHAPTER 3   WORKING WITH RELATIONAL DATA ON AZURE

```sql
-- With sorting
SELECT * FROM Employees ORDER BY LastName;

-- With aggregation
SELECT Department, COUNT(*)
FROM Employees
GROUP BY Department;
```

3. DML (Data Manipulation Language)

It modifies data within tables.

Commands

- INSERT: Adds new records
- UPDATE: Modifies existing records
- DELETE: Removes records
- MERGE: Upsert operation

Example:

```sql
-- Insert data
INSERT INTO Employees
VALUES (1, 'John', 'Doe', 'IT', 'john@example.com');

-- Update data
UPDATE Employees
SET Department = 'HR'
WHERE EmployeeID = 1;

-- Delete data
DELETE FROM Employees
WHERE EmployeeID = 1;
```

4. DCL (Data Control Language)

It controls access to data.
Commands

- GRANT: Gives privileges
- REVOKE: Removes privileges
- DENY: Explicitly denies permissions

Example:

```
-- Grant select permission
GRANT SELECT ON Employees TO user1;

-- Revoke update permission
REVOKE UPDATE ON Employees FROM user1;

-- Deny delete permission
DENY DELETE ON Employees TO user1;
```

5. TCL (Transaction Control Language)

It manages database transactions.
Commands

- COMMIT: Saves changes permanently
- ROLLBACK: Undoes changes
- SAVEPOINT: Sets a point to roll back to
- SET TRANSACTION: Configures transaction properties

Example:

```
BEGIN TRANSACTION;
    UPDATE Accounts SET balance = balance - 100
    WHERE account_id = 1;
```

```
UPDATE Accounts SET balance = balance + 100
WHERE account_id = 2;

-- If everything is OK
COMMIT;

-- If error occurs
-- ROLLBACK;
```

The Structured Query Language (SQL) is a powerful method of accessing relational database engines across multiple platforms. Although the underlying SQL syntax is mostly universal, each DBMS implements its own extensions and optimizations. It is an essential aspect for anyone who aims to manage a database effectively or develop applications.

Explore Database

1. Tables

To architect your data in a tabular format – i.e., to lay it down in the form of tables, which are the primary storage entities in any relational systems – the data is split into verticals, which we refer to as columns or fields, and horizontals, which we refer to as rows or records.

Key Features

- Store structured data
- Enforce data integrity with constraints (PK, FK, UNIQUE, NOT NULL)
- Support data types (INT, VARCHAR, DATE, etc.)

Example:

```
-- Creating a table
CREATE TABLE Employees (
    EmployeeID INT PRIMARY KEY,
```

```
    FirstName VARCHAR(50) NOT NULL,
    LastName VARCHAR(50) NOT NULL,
    HireDate DATE,
    Salary DECIMAL(10,2),
    DepartmentID INT,
    CONSTRAINT FK_Department FOREIGN KEY (DepartmentID)
    REFERENCES Departments(DepartmentID)
);

-- Inserting data
INSERT INTO Employees VALUES
(1, 'Naveen', 'Kumar', '2020-01-15', 75000.00, 101),
(2, 'Will', 'Smith', '2019-05-22', 82000.00, 102);
```

2. Views

Views are virtual tables that represent the result of a stored SQL query.

Key Features

- Simplify complex queries
- Provide security by restricting column access
- Don't store data physically (except materialized views)

Example:

```
-- Creating a view
CREATE VIEW IT_Employees AS
SELECT EmployeeID, FirstName, LastName, HireDate
FROM Employees
WHERE DepartmentID = 101;   -- IT Department

-- Using the view
SELECT * FROM IT_Employees;
```

3. Functions

Functions are reusable database objects that perform operations and return a single value or a table.

Types

- **Scalar Functions**: Return a single value
- **Table-Valued Functions**: Return a result set

Example (Scalar Function):

```
-- Creating a function
CREATE FUNCTION GetEmployeeAge(@EmployeeID INT)
RETURNS INT
AS
BEGIN
    DECLARE @Age INT;
    SELECT @Age = DATEDIFF(YEAR, BirthDate, GETDATE())
    FROM Employees
    WHERE EmployeeID = @EmployeeID;
    RETURN @Age;
END;

-- Using the function
SELECT dbo.GetEmployeeAge(1) AS EmployeeAge;
```

Example (Table-Valued Function):

```
CREATE FUNCTION GetDepartmentEmployees(@DeptID INT)
RETURNS TABLE
AS
RETURN (
```

```
    SELECT EmployeeID, FirstName, LastName
    FROM Employees
    WHERE DepartmentID = @DeptID
);

-- Using the function
SELECT * FROM dbo.GetDepartmentEmployees(101);
```

5. Indexes

Indexes are database objects that improve data retrieval speed by creating optimized access paths.

Types

- **Clustered Index**: Determines physical order of data (one per table)
- **Non-clustered Index**: Separate structure with pointers to data
- **Unique Index**: Enforces uniqueness
- **Composite Index**: On multiple columns

Example:

```
-- Creating a clustered index (usually on PK)
CREATE CLUSTERED INDEX IX_Employees_EmployeeID
ON Employees(EmployeeID);

-- Creating a non-clustered index
CREATE NONCLUSTERED INDEX IX_Employees_Department
ON Employees(DepartmentID);

-- Creating a composite index
CREATE INDEX IX_Employees_Name
ON Employees(LastName, FirstName);
```

```
-- Creating a unique index
CREATE UNIQUE INDEX IX_Employees_Email
ON Employees(Email);
```

Comparison of Database Objects

The key comparison between various database objects in terms of purpose, storage, update frequency, and performance impact is presented in Table 3-1.

Table 3-1. Database Object Comparison

Object Type	Purpose	Storage	Update Frequency	Performane Impact
Table	Data storage	Physical	High	N/A
View	Virtual table representation	Logical (query)	Dynamic	Depends on base table
Function	Return computed values	Logical	Reusable	Varies by complexity
Stored Procedure	Execute business logic	Logical	Reusable	High (pre-compiled)
Index	Speed up queries	Physical	Updated on DML	High (read speed)

A database is a structured collection of objects designed to efficiently store and process data. These objects include tables, hold raw data, views are used to clarify access to that data, functions and procedures automate processes, and indexes speed up searches. Understanding these concepts is key to making optimized, secure, and performant systems around databases.

Azure Relational Data Services
Overview

SQL Server workloads in the cloud contain a set of fully managed and self-managed Azure services. These services provide different degrees of control, compatibility, and management based on business requirements.

Azure SQL Family
1. Azure SQL Database

It is a serverless, intelligent, and scalable version of the SQL Database with built-in high availability, security, and automatic tuning.

Ideal for: Modern cloud applications and automated management

2. Azure SQL Managed Instance

It is a bridge between SQL Server and Azure SQL Database, offering close to 100% SQL compatibility (common language) across on-premises SQL Server.

Ideal for: Lift-and-shift migrations that need less modification

3. SQL Server on Azure Virtual Machines (VMs)

SQL Server installed on Azure Virtual Machines, where you are responsible for managing both the SQL Server instance and the underlying operating system.

Ideal for: Behind-the-times applications requiring full control over SQL Server

CHAPTER 3   WORKING WITH RELATIONAL DATA ON AZURE

Comparison of Azure SQL Services

The key differences among Azure SQL Database, Azure SQL Managed Instance, and SQL Server on Azure Virtual Machines in terms of cloud service type, SQL Server compatibility, architecture, high availability, maintenance and patching, scalability, security, use cases, pricing model, and networking are presented in Table 3-2.

Table 3-2. Azure SQL Services Comparison

Feature	Azure SQL Database	Azure SQL Managed Instance	SQL Server on Azure VMs
Type of Cloud Service	Fully managed PaaS	Nearly fully managed PaaS	Self-managed IaaS
SQL Server Compatibility	Latest features, some limitations	Near 100% compatibility	Full compatibility
Architecture	Single database or elastic pool	Instance-level isolation	Full VM control (OS + SQL)
High Availability	Built-in (99.99% SLA)	Built-in (99.99% SLA)	Customer configured (requires Always On)
Maintenance and Patching	Fully automated	Fully automated	Manual (customer responsibility)
Scalability	Auto-scaling (serverless option)	Manual scaling	Manual scaling (VM resizing)
Security	Built-in threat detection, encryption	Advanced security features	Customer-managed security

(continued)

Table 3-2. (*continued*)

Feature	Azure SQL Database	Azure SQL Managed Instance	SQL Server on Azure VMs
Use Cases	Cloud-native apps, SaaS solutions	Lift-and-shift migrations, enterprise apps	Legacy apps, full control needed
Pricing Model	DTU/vCore, serverless	vCore based	VM + SQL licensing costs
Networking	Public endpoint, private link	VNet integration required	Full VNet customization

Key Features of Azure SQL Services

1. Azure SQL Database

- Serverless compute option (auto-pauses when it is not in use)
- Hyperscale (extreme scalability, up to 100TB+)
- AI built-in performance tuning
- High availability with the zone redundant

2. Azure SQL Managed Instance

- Almost 100% compatible with SQL Server
- Instance-level isolation (e.g., on-prem SQL Server)
- Support for virtual network (VNet) native
- Cross-database queries and SQL Agent

3. SQL Server on Azure VMs

- Operating system (OS, SQL settings) full administrative control
- Fully integrated with all SQL Server features (SSIS, SSRS, SSAS)
- Bring Your Own License (BYOL) or pay-as-you-go
- Individualized backup and disaster recovery solutions

Business Benefits of Azure Relational Data Services

1. Azure SQL Database Benefits

Cost Efficiency

- Lower operational expenses (no hardware/software maintenance)
- Serverless option (pay per active usage, auto-pauses during periods of inactivity)
- Inherent high availability (LLD DR configurations are unnecessary)

Performance and Scalability

- Automatic performance tuning (optimization driven by AI)
- Hyperscale support (expands to 100TB+ with no downtime)
- Elastic pools (cost-efficient allocation of resources to databases)

CHAPTER 3 WORKING WITH RELATIONAL DATA ON AZURE

Security and Compliance

- Integrated threat detection (detects SQL injections, brute-force attacks)
- Always Encrypted (helps encrypt sensitive data in use and at rest)
- Compliance certifications (GDPR, HIPAA, ISO 27001)

Business Agility

- Quick provision (minutes)
- Global scalability (deploy to Azure regions)
- Integration with other Azure services (Power BI, Azure Functions, Logic Apps)

2. Azure SQL Managed Instance Benefits

Migration Simplicity

- Near 100% compatibility with on-prem SQL Server (low code changes)
- Lift-and-shift ready (supports SQL Agent, cross-db queries)
- Native VNet integration (secure connectivity like on-prem)

Enterprise-Grade Features

- Instance isolation (dedicated resources, no noisy neighbors)
- Business-critical tier (99.995% SLA with added replica failover)
- Point-in-time restore (recover against accidental deletions)

Hybrid Cloud Flexibility

- Linked Server support (connect to on-prem data sources)
- Distributed transactions (operations at multiple databases consistently)
- Shard instance pools (saves cost for small workloads)

3. SQL Server on Azure VMs Benefits

Full Control and Customization

- Full admin rights (tool level, OS, SQL Server settings, third-party tools)
- Full support for every SQL component (SSIS, SSRS, SSAS, R/Python)
- Bring Your Own License (BYOL) (using existing SQL Server licenses)

Legacy Application Support

- No changes in the application (suitable for "no-touch" migrations)
- Custom backup/DR solutions (business oriented)
- Resource dedicated (guaranteed processing for mission-critical applications)

Cost Optimization

- Reserved Instances (save up to 72% on long-term workloads)
- Hybrid Benefit (up to 55% off for reusing on-prem licenses)
- Shutdown/startup VMs (control costs for non-production stacks)

Comparative Business Benefits Summary

The key business benefits of Azure SQL Database, Azure SQL Managed Instance, and SQL Server on Azure Virtual Machines in terms of cost savings, migration ease, management overhead, high availability, security, legacy support, and global scaling are presented in Table 3-3.

Table 3-3. Azure SQL Services Business Benefits

Business Need	Azure SQL Database	Azure SQL Managed Instance	SQL Server on VMs
Cost Savings	Pay-as-you-go, auto-scaling	License-included pricing	BYOL and Hybrid Benefit
Migration Ease	May require app changes	Near-zero code changes	No changes needed
Management Overhead	Fully automated	Mostly automated	Self-managed
High Availability	99.99% SLA built-in	99.99% SLA built-in	Customer configured
Security	Built-in encryption and threat detection	Enterprise security features	Customer managed
Legacy Support	Limited	SQL Agent, linked servers	Full feature support
Global Scaling	Multi-region deploy	Limited to single region	Complex to scale

Microsoft Azure has options like Azure SQL Database for cloud-native, scalable environments, Azure SQL Managed Instance for easy migration, and SQL Server on VMs for legacy support and full control. Each service comes with its own benefits such as pricing, ease of management, compatibility, and scalability, offering businesses the option to select the service that best suits their workloads.

Open Source Relational Databases on Azure

Enterprises rely on data today, and they require dependable, scalable, and cost-effective database solutions. Open source relational databases such as MySQL, MariaDB, and PostgreSQL have gained popularity for their flexibility, performance, and community support. These databases are also available as fully managed services from Microsoft Azure as Azure Database for MySQL, Azure Database for MariaDB, and Azure Database for PostgreSQL, leveraging the best of open source technologies integrated with Microsoft Azure's cloud benefits like high availability, security, and auto-scaling.

Overview of Services

MySQL

MySQL is one of the most often used open source relational databases, originally developed by MySQL AB, and is now owned by Oracle. MySQL is known for its fast performance, dependability, and ease of use, making it one of the most popular databases for web applications, especially in the LAMP stack (Linux, Apache, MySQL, and PHP/Python/Perl). MySQL supports full ACID compliance through its InnoDB storage engine and supports replication, partitioning, and full-text search. It is often applied in ecommerce, content management systems (such as WordPress and Drupal), and Online Transaction Processing (OLTP) applications.

MariaDB

MySQL was forked into a community version called MariaDB by the original developers of MySQL, shortly after Oracle's acquisition raised alarms. It also remains highly compatible with MySQL, so you can switch most applications from MySQL to MariaDB without changing any code.

CHAPTER 3   WORKING WITH RELATIONAL DATA ON AZURE

MariaDB provides performance improvements, new storage engines (like Aria, ColumnStore), and better scalability. This is commonly used for data warehousing, analytics, and high-performance web applications.

PostgreSQL

PostgreSQL (or Postgres) is an advanced open source object-relational database system that is known for its robustness, extensibility, and standards compliance. PostgreSQL, unlike MySQL and MariaDB, supports complex queries, JSON/document storage, geospatial data (PostGIS), and custom functions in several programming languages (Python, R, PL/pgSQL). It is best suited for applications having high concurrency, large-scale data processing, and enterprise-level features, including, but not limited to, financial systems, geospatial applications, and AI/ML data pipelines.

Azure Managed Open Source Database Services

Azure offers fully managed versions of these databases, meaning that infrastructure management is taken care of, while providing high availability, security, and scalability.

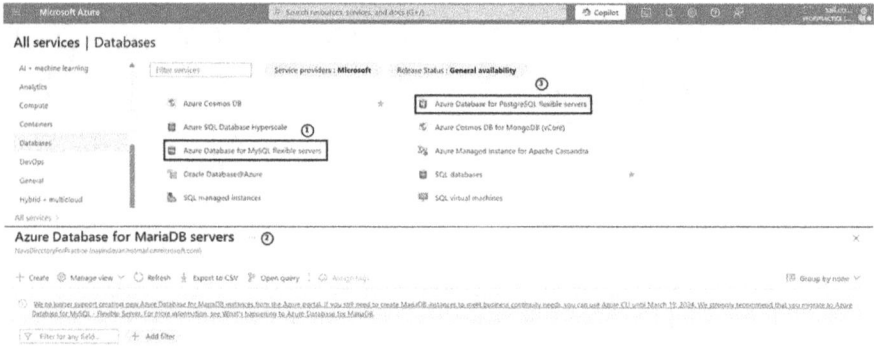

Figure 3-3. *Azure Open Source Database Services*

CHAPTER 3   WORKING WITH RELATIONAL DATA ON AZURE

Figure 3-3 shows the Azure open source database services; the services are labeled as 1, 2, and 3. Each of these services is explained below.

1. Azure Database for MySQL

- A PaaS (Platform-as-a-Service) offering with support for both Single Server (legacy) and Flexible Server (recommended) deployments

- Includes automated backup, scale, and HA (99.99% SLA)

- Best for web applications, SaaS platforms, and OLTP (Online Transaction Processing)

2. Azure Database for MariaDB

- A managed service for MariaDB workloads, though Microsoft advises migrating to MySQL Flexible Server as that service is being retired

- Compatible with bare minimum high availability and VNet integration

3. Azure Database for PostgreSQL

- Provides Single Server (legacy), Flexible Server (preferred), and Hyperscale (Citus) for distributed workloads

- Supports advanced data types (JSON, GIS), AI/ML integration, and horizontal scaling

- Best suited for enterprise applications, real-time analytics, and geospatial systems

Benefits of Azure Managed Open Source Databases

Benefits of Azure Database for MySQL

You get the following enterprise-grade features with Azure Database for MySQL:

- Create high availability with automatic failover out of the box
- Predictable, consistent performance across workloads
- On-demand elastic scaling that automatically adjusts to the demand
- End-to-end security with data encryption at rest and in transit
- Automated backups with 35-day point-in-time restore
- Large enterprise compliance with worldwide security standards
- Economical price costs with pay-as-you-go model

A full set of monitoring functionality with various alerts, performance metrics, and diagnostics is available for Azure Database for MySQL.

Benefits of Azure Database for MariaDB

Azure Database for MariaDB provides

- High availability architecture – included at no extra cost
- Transparent pricing with proven delivery
- Pay only for what you need, with instant scaling to align with workload demands

CHAPTER 3   WORKING WITH RELATIONAL DATA ON AZURE

- Military-grade security safeguarding data at rest and in motion

- Protection for backup using migration automation, with a 35-day restoration period

- Enterprise security controls and compliance certifications

Important *Microsoft encourages users to transition to Azure Database for MySQL Flexible Server in order to receive continued support and improved capabilities.*

Benefits of Azure Database for PostgreSQL

Azure Database for PostgreSQL delivers

- Smart high availability with automatic failover

- Well-known PostgreSQL experience, pgAdmin compatible

- Improved monitoring via azure_sys query tracking

- Built-in protections to ensure enterprise-grade security

- Flexible deployment – Hyperscale (Citus)

- International compliance standards for regulated industries

PgAdmin can be used for your database maintenance, but Azure Managed Service handles the backend server maintenance operations backups automatically. The Query Store, including views like get_mfe_qs_view_qs, provides insights for performance tuning.

CHAPTER 3 WORKING WITH RELATIONAL DATA ON AZURE

Summary

This chapter introduced fundamental principles of relational databases on Azure, discussing

1. **Relational Data Fundamentals**
   - What tables, rows, and columns are
   - Keys and relationships: primary key and foreign key
   - Advantages of normalization (1NF, 2NF, 3NF)

2. **SQL and Database Management**
   - SQL commands (DDL, DML, DQL, DCL, TCL)
   - Common variants of SQL (MySQL, PostgreSQL, SQL Server)

3. **Database Objects**
   - Tables, views, stored procedures, functions, and indexes

4. **Azure SQL Services**
   - Azure SQL Database (PaaS for cloud-native apps)
   - Azure SQL Managed Instance (almost 100% of SQL Server compatibility)
   - SQL Server on Azure VMs (complete control for legacy workloads)

5. **Open Source Databases on Azure**
   - MySQL, MariaDB, and PostgreSQL overview
   - Azure services management for each with out-of-the-box HA, security, and scaling

6. **Business Benefits of Azure Manager Open Source Database**

    - Reduced management overhead

    - Industrial security and compliance

    - On-demand scalability and cost efficiency

In this chapter, you learned about relational databases in Azure, including how to choose a suitable service for different workloads.

CHAPTER 4

Exploring Non-relational Data on Azure

In this chapter, you will also learn about non-relational data modalities and how they differ from relational data. These range from JSON documents for schema-less data structures to a myriad of key-value pairs for fast lookups to graph data for complex relationships.

This chapter walks you through Azure's storage services, from Azure Blob Storage for unstructured data such as media files, Azure Data Lake Storage Gen2 for big data analytics, Microsoft OneLake for keeping all data in one place within Fabric, Azure File Storage for shared file systems, and Azure Table Storage as simple NoSQL key-value storage. You will learn about their characteristics and when to use each one depending on various performance, scale, and access pattern requirements.

Additionally, the chapter introduces Azure Cosmos DB, a massively powerful multi-model database service that offers simple and fast global scalability with low latency. Learn about key features such as automatic indexing, turnkey global distribution, and SLAs that ensure high availability.

CHAPTER 4   EXPLORING NON-RELATIONAL DATA ON AZURE

In this chapter, we will cover the various APIs it provides, including

- Core (SQL) for document data
- MongoDB for MongoDB compatibility
- Cassandra for column-family data
- Gremlin for graph traversals
- Table for key-value scenarios
- PostgreSQL for distributed relational workloads

We will also cover real-world use cases for Azure Cosmos DB, including globally distributed apps, IoT telemetry management, real-time recommendation engines, and high-speed gaming leaderboards. The following examples should give you a sense of when to use this service for different use cases that require massive scale and performance.

Finally, by the end of this chapter, you will have a recovery method from non-relational data, and your storage services will be available on Azure for various unstructured data needs, and you will discover how you can use the multi-model solution of Azure Cosmos DB for managing and working with different Renaissance and citizen data types that you need to go hybrid or cloud-native in your applications.

Introduction to Non-relational Data Overview

Non-relational data has become a key part of modern applications due to the growth of unstructured and semi-structured data. Social media content, IoT telemetry data, JSON documents, multimedia files – a motley collection of diverse data types that do not conform to classical tabular schemas.

Non-relational Data

Non-relational data, also known as NoSQL data, is a type of database built for various types of data models apart from tables, like documents, graphs, or key-value pairs. While traditional RDBMS focuses on strict data structures, non-relational databases are built for flexibility, scalability, and performance in today's applications.

Key Characteristics

- **Schema Flexibility**: No fixed schema; structures evolve with application needs.

- **Scalability**: Horizontal scaling (distributing data across servers) for massive workloads.

- **Data Models**: Supports documents, key-value, graph, and column-family formats.

- **Use Cases**: Ideal for unstructured/semi-structured data (e.g., social media, IoT), real-time apps, and global-scale solutions.

Why Non-relational on Azure?

Azure provides managed services like Azure Cosmos DB and Blob Storage to handle non-relational data efficiently, enabling developers to focus on innovation rather than infrastructure.

CHAPTER 4   EXPLORING NON-RELATIONAL DATA ON AZURE

Difference Between Relational and Non-relational Data

The key differences between relational and non-relational data in terms of data model, schema, storage, query language, scalability, consistency model, transactions, examples, and use cases are shown in Table 4-1.

Table 4-1. Difference Between Relational and Non-relational Data

Feature	Relation Data	Non-relational Data
Data Model	Tabular (rows and columns)	Flexible, varies by type (documents, key-value, etc.)
Schema	Fixed schema (predefined structure)	Schema-less or flexible schema
Storage	Tables in relational databases (SQL)	Collections, documents, blobs, etc.
Query Language	SQL	Varies: NoSQL, JSON queries, API-based
Scalability	Vertical scaling (upgrading server hardware)	Horizontal scaling (adding servers)
Consistency Model	ACID (strong consistency)	BASE (eventual consistency)
Transactions	Complex multi-row transactions	Limited to single document/entity
Examples	SQL Server, PostgreSQL, MySQL	Azure Cosmos DB, MongoDB, Cassandra, Azure Blob Storage
Use Case	Structured data, complex joins	Unstructured or semi-structured, hierarchical, or varied

When to Choose Non-relational Data?

- Data is changing rapidly or has no consistent schema.
- Need for flexible data formats (e.g., JSON, XML).
- Real-time or large-scale ingestion of telemetry data.
- High-velocity and high-volume data processing (e.g., logs, clickstreams).

Examples of Non-relational Data

Understanding the different types of non-relational data helps determine which Azure service to use. Below are the common types.

1. Key-Value

- Data is stored as key-value pairs.
- Extremely fast for read/write operations.
- Common in caching, session storage, and real-time lookups.
- **Azure Service**: Azure Cosmos DB (Key-Value API), Azure Cache for Redis.

2. Document

- Stores data in formats like JSON, BSON (Binary JSON), or XML.
  - BSON (Binary JSON) is a binary-encoded serialization format that extends JSON with support for additional data types and faster processing.

- Flexible schema allows each document to have a different structure.
- Ideal for content management systems, product catalogs, and user profiles.
- **Azure Service**: Azure Cosmos DB (API for MongoDB, SQL API), Azure Document DB (legacy).

3. Column-Family

- Data is stored in columns rather than rows.
- Optimized for read-heavy workloads and high performance over wide datasets.
- Used in time-series data, recommendation engines, and analytics.
- **Azure Service**: Azure Cosmos DB (Cassandra API), Apache HBase on HDInsight.

4. Graph

- Data is modeled as nodes and edges with properties.
- Useful for modeling relationships and interconnected data (e.g., social networks, fraud detection).
- **Azure Service**: Azure Cosmos DB (Gremlin API).

5. Object (Blob Storage)

- Stores unstructured binary data like images, videos, backups, and logs.
- Best for large-scale storage and analytics on raw data.
- **Azure Service**: Azure Blob Storage.

CHAPTER 4   EXPLORING NON-RELATIONAL DATA ON AZURE

Azure Storage Services
Explore Azure Blob Storage
Introduction to Azure Blob Storage

Azure Blob Storage is Microsoft's cloud object storage solution. It is optimized for storing large quantities of unstructured data – data that does not follow a formal data model or definition, including text, binary files, images, videos, backups, and logs. The term "Blob" refers to Binary Large Object, and Azure Blob Storage is a foundational service designed to provide scalable, durable, and secure storage for this type of data.

Blob Storage is ideal for

- Serving images or documents directly to a browser
- Storing files for distributed access
- Streaming video and audio
- Writing to log files
- Storing data for backup, disaster recovery, and archiving
- Storing data for analysis by an on-premises or Azure-hosted service

Types of Blobs in Azure Blob Storage

Azure Blob Storage supports three distinct types of blobs, each designed for different use cases.

1. Block Blobs

Best for

- Storing text and binary data like documents, media files, backups, etc.
- Data is broken into blocks (up to 100 MB per block), each identified by a block ID.
- You can upload or modify individual blocks before committing the whole blob.

Use Case Examples

- Storing images, videos, and PDFs for a website
- Uploading large files in parallel (efficient for large media content)

2. Page Blobs

Best for

- Frequent read/write operations and random access patterns.
- Used primarily for Azure virtual machine disks (VHD files).
- Data is organized into 512-byte pages for efficient I/O.

Use Case Examples

- Azure VM operating system and data disks
- Databases or applications requiring high-performance random reads/writes

3. Append Blobs

Best for

- Append-only operations (data is only added, not modified)
- Optimized for use cases where data is continuously appended

Use Case Examples

- Logging from applications or IoT devices
- Audit trails and telemetry collection

Azure Blob Storage Access Tiers

To help manage cost and performance, Azure Blob Storage provides **three access tiers** for storing blob data. The characteristics of Azure Blob Storage access tiers – Hot, Cool, and Archive – in terms of description, performance and cost, common use cases, and data availability are shown in Table 4-2.

These tiers allow you to balance between **cost** and **access frequency**.

Table 4-2. Azure Blob Storage Access Tiers

Access Tier	Description	Performance and Cost	Common Use Cases	Data Availability
Hot	Default tier for frequently accessed data. Stored on high-performance media	Highest performance Higher storage cost Lower access cost	Active files, media, real-time data processing	Data is available **immediately** (low latency in milliseconds)
Cool	For infrequently accessed data. Suitable for data that becomes less active over time	Lower performance than Hot Lower storage cost Higher access cost	Backups, older documents, staging inactive data before archiving	Data is available **immediately** (slightly higher latency than Hot)
Archive	Designed for rarely accessed historical data. Data is offline and must be rehydrated before use	Lowest storage cost Highest access cost High latency	Compliance data, archived logs, long-term backups	Data is **offline**; retrieval can take **hours** (rehydration required)

Real-World Use Cases

Real-world use cases of Azure Blobs in terms of scenario, type of blob, tier, and description are shown in Table 4-3.

Table 4-3. *Azure Blob Real-World Use Cases*

Scenario	Type of Blob	Tier	Description
Storing product images and manuals for an ecommerce site	Block Blob	Hot	Frequently accessed assets delivered to users via a CDN
Application logging for microservices	Append Blob	Cool	Logs written continually but accessed only during debugging or audits
VM operating system disk	Page Blob	NA	Mounted as a disk on an Azure Virtual Machine
Archiving employee records for regulatory compliance	Block Blob	Archive	Stored for years, accessed only when needed
Backing up database snapshots weekly	Block Blob	Cool	Infrequent restore operations, with life cycle rules to move to archive
IoT telemetry ingestion	Append Blob	Hot/Cool	Real-time stream stored in append format for later analysis

Explore Azure Data Lake Storage Gen2

Introduction to Azure Data Lake Storage Gen2

Azure Data Lake Storage Gen2 (ADLS Gen2) is the next generation of Azure Data Lake Storage for big data analytics workloads built on Azure Blob Storage hyperscale data lake solution. It builds on the strengths of Azure Blob Storage, incorporating benefits such as scalability and cost-efficiency, while also providing a hierarchical namespace that supports a file system structure (directory, subdirectory, and file). ADLS Gen2 is designed for analytics frameworks like Apache Spark, Hadoop, and Azure Synapse Analytics, making it ubiquitous within modern data architectures.

Key Features

- **Hierarchical Namespace**: Organize data into folders and subfolders (unlike Blob Storage's flat structure)
- **POSIX Compliance**: Supports POSIX permissions for fine-grained access control
- **Multi-protocol Access**: Access data via **Blob APIs** (for existing apps) and **Azure Data Lake Storage REST APIs** (for analytics)
- **Massive Scalability**: Store exabytes of data with petabyte-scale throughput
- **Integration**: Native compatibility with Azure analytics services (e.g., Azure Databricks, Synapse Analytics)

Core Components of ADLS Gen2

1. **Hierarchical Namespace**
   - Enables directory-level operations (create, rename, delete) and atomic file updates.
   - For example, organize raw, processed, and curated data in folders like /raw/sales/2023.

2. **Optimized for Analytics**
   - Supports ACID transactions for reliable data processing.
   - Columnar data formats (Parquet, Delta Lake) are stored efficiently for fast querying.

3. **Security**

    - **Role-Based Access Control (RBAC)**: Manage permissions at the storage account, directory, or file level.

    - **Azure Active Directory (AAD) Integration**: Securely authenticate users and services.

4. **Cost Efficiency**

    - Leverages Blob Storage's access tiers (Hot, Cool, Archive) for cost optimization.

Why Use ADLS Gen2 over Blob Storage for Analytics?

The comparison between Azure Blob Storage and Azure Data Lake Storage Gen2 in terms of various aspects is shown in Table 4-4.

Table 4-4. ADLS Gen2 over Blob Storage

Aspect	Blob Storage	ADLS Gen2
Data Organization	Flat namespace	Hierarchical namespace with folders and files
Big Data Compatibility	Limited	Full support (HDFS compatible)
File Operations	Expensive or not natively supported	Native support for rename, move, delete, etc.
Analytics Integration	Not optimized for analytics	Designed for high-performance analytics workloads
Security Model	Azure RBAC only	Azure RBAC + POSIX ACLs

Use Cases for Azure Data Lake Storage Gen2

1. **Enterprise Data Lake**

    - Central repository for structured, semi-structured, and unstructured data.

    - **Example**: A retail company ingests sales transactions (CSV), social media feeds (JSON), and customer call recordings (audio) into ADLS Gen2 for unified analytics.

2. **Real-Time Analytics**

    - Stream IoT or telemetry data into ADLS Gen2 and analyze it in near real time.

    - **Example**: A manufacturing plant uses Azure Stream Analytics to write sensor data to ADLS Gen2, then trains predictive maintenance models with Azure Machine Learning.

3. **Machine Learning Pipelines**

    - Store training datasets in Parquet format for fast access by ML frameworks.

    - **Example**: A healthcare provider uses ADLS Gen2 to store anonymized patient data, which is processed by Azure Databricks to train disease prediction models.

4. **Log and Event Analytics**

    - Ingest application logs or clickstream data for troubleshooting and user behavior analysis.

    - **Example**: A gaming company stores player event logs in ADLS Gen2 and uses Synapse Analytics to identify gameplay trends.

Integration with Other Azure Services

- **Azure Synapse Analytics**: Run big data queries directly on files stored in ADLS Gen2.

- **Azure Data Factory**: Use ADF pipelines to ingest, transform, and orchestrate data movement.

- **Azure Databricks**: Read and write to ADLS Gen2 using Spark for scalable analytics.

- **Power BI**: Connect to curated and transformed data from ADLS Gen2 for visualization.

- **Azure Purview (Microsoft Purview)**: Perform data discovery, cataloging, and lineage tracking.

Explore Microsoft OneLake in Fabric

Introduction to Microsoft OneLake

OneLake is a unified logical data lake within Microsoft Fabric that acts as the single storage layer for every analytics workload across an organization. Compared to traditional data lakes that require you to manage disparate, siloed repositories, OneLake offers the "OneDrive for data" experience, allowing for easy collaboration, governance, and scale.

Key Features

- **Unified Storage**: A single logical data lake for all data (structured, semi-structured, unstructured)

- **Integrated with Fabric**: Provisioned automatically with every Microsoft Fabric workspace, no setup needed

- **Open Data Formats**: Based on Delta Parquet and compatible with open source analytic tools (i.e., Spark, Pandas)
- **Shortcuts**: Possible to virtualize data from third-party sources (i.e., Azure Data Lake Storage, Amazon S3) without having to duplicate it
- **Governance**: Unified security, lineage, and discovery with Microsoft Purview integration
- **Multi-cloud Support**: Connect to data across Azure, AWS, and Google Cloud

Why OneLake?

In Fabric, OneLake allows analytics, machine learning, and business intelligence workflows by eliminating data silos by consolidating data from various sources into a logical layer.

Core Concepts of OneLake

1. **Logical Data Lake**
   - A unified, virtualized storage layer that wraps physical storage (i.e., Azure Blob storage) transpiring among workspaces.
   - For instance, data engineers and analysts will be accessing the same OneLake storage from Fabric's Synapse Data Engineering and Power BI.
2. **Delta Lake Foundation**
   - Delta Lake format (Parquet-based) type data storage supports ACID transaction, schema enforcement, and time travel.

CHAPTER 4   EXPLORING NON-RELATIONAL DATA ON AZURE

3. **Shortcuts**

    - Linking to data sources in external storage without data copy (ADLS Gen2, AWS S3, etc.).

    - For example, a shortcut to an Azure SQL Database table surfaces itself as a Delta table in OneLake.

4. **Workspaces**

    - Data in OneLake is organized into Fabric workspaces, which serve as collaborative workspaces for teams.

5. **Security**

    - **Role-Based Access Control (RBAC):** Set permissions at the workspace, folder, or file level.

    - **Microsoft Entra ID (Azure AD):** Unified authentication for users and services.

Use Cases for Microsoft OneLake

1. **Enterprise-Wide Data Sharing**

    - Centralize sales, marketing, and supply chain data in OneLake for cross-departmental analytics.

    - **Example:** A financial institution consolidates transaction logs, customer profiles, and risk models in OneLake for fraud detection.

2. **Self-Service Analytics**

    - Business user's access pre-curated datasets in OneLake via Power BI without relying on IT.

    - **Example:** Marketing teams analyze campaign performance using Delta tables stored in OneLake.

3. **Real-Time Insights**

    - Stream IoT data into OneLake and process it with Fabric's Real-Time Analytics.

    - **Example**: A logistics company monitors fleet telemetry in real time and predicts delivery delays.

4. **AI/ML Workflows**

    - Train machine learning models on Delta tables in OneLake using Fabric's Data Science tools.

    - **Example**: A healthcare provider uses OneLake data to predict patient readmission risks.

Integration with Microsoft Fabric Tools

- **Synapse Data Engineering**: Transform raw data into Delta tables using Spark notebooks.

- **Data Factory**: Ingest data from 200+ connectors into OneLake.

- **Power BI**: Build reports directly on OneLake datasets.

- **Data Science**: Train ML models with OneLake data using Python/R.

- **Data Warehouse**: Query OneLake data using T-SQL in Fabric's serverless Data Warehouse.

CHAPTER 4 EXPLORING NON-RELATIONAL DATA ON AZURE

Explore Azure File Storage

Introduction to Azure File Storage

Azure File Storage is a fully managed file share in the cloud, compatible with industry standard protocols such as SMB (Server Message Block) and NFS (Network File System). It supports consistent and detailed data access across hybrid or cloud-native scenarios, including legacy application migrations, collaborative workspaces, and lift-and-shift workloads.

Key Features

- **Cross-Platform Compatibility**: Accessible from Windows, Linux, and macOS systems
- **Fully Managed**: No hardware provisioning or patching required
- **Scalability**: Scale storage capacity and performance independently
- **Integration:** Mount file shares to Azure VMs, on-premises servers, or serverless apps
- **Security**: Supports encryption at rest and in transit, Azure AD/AD DS authentication (SMB), and virtual network (VNet) isolation

Supported Network File Sharing Protocols

Azure File Storage supports two protocols for file sharing, each tailored to specific operating systems and use cases as shown in Table 4-5.

115

Table 4-5. *Network File Sharing Protocol Types*

Protocol	Description	Requirements
SMB (Server Message Block)	Industry standard protocol for Windows file sharing, also supported by Linux/macOS via SMB clients	**Standard or Premium tier** storage accounts **Azure AD or Active Directory Domain Services (AD DS)** for identity-based access
NFS (Network File System)	Protocol commonly used in Unix/Linux environments for high-performance file sharing	**Premium tier** storage account **Virtual network (VNet)** configuration to control access. NFS clients (Linux/macOS)

Key Differences

- **SMB** is ideal for hybrid environments (e.g., Windows-based applications).
- **NFS** is preferred for Linux workloads requiring POSIX-compliant file systems (e.g., high-performance computing).

Deployment Considerations

1. Storage Account Tiers

- **Premium Tier**
    - Required for **NFS shares**
    - Offers low latency, high throughput, and IOPS for performance-sensitive workloads
    - Billed per provisioned capacity (GB)

CHAPTER 4   EXPLORING NON-RELATIONAL DATA ON AZURE

- **Standard Tier**
  - Supports **SMB shares** only
  - Cost-effective for general-purpose file sharing
  - Billed per used capacity (GB)

2. Network Configuration

- **SMB**
  - Accessible over public internet (with SAS tokens) or private endpoints
  - Integrates with Azure AD or AD DS for user-level permissions
- **NFS**
  - **Requires VNet peering or private endpoints** for secure access.
  - Public internet access is disabled by default for NFS shares.

3. Redundancy Options

- **Locally Redundant Storage (LRS)**: Data replicated within a single data center
- **Zone-Redundant Storage (ZRS)**: Replicates across availability zones for higher resilience
- **Geo-redundant Storage (GRS)**: Cross-region replication for disaster recovery

Use Cases and Examples

1. Hybrid Cloud File Sharing (SMB)

- **Scenario**: A company migrates an on-premises Windows application to Azure VMs but retains a file share for configuration files.
- **Solution**: Use **SMB file shares** to maintain compatibility with existing scripts and tools.

2. Lift-and-Shift Linux Workloads (NFS)

- **Scenario**: A research team runs a genomics analysis tool on Linux VMs, requiring shared access to large datasets.
- **Solution**: Deploy **NFS shares** on Premium tier for POSIX compliance and high throughput.

3. Collaborative Development Environments

- **Scenario**: Developers across Windows and macOS machines need shared access to source code.
- **Solution**: Mount an **SMB file share** to all machines using Azure AD credentials.

4. Backup and Archival

- **Scenario**: An organization backs up user home directories to Azure File Storage.
- **Solution**: Use **Cool tier** SMB shares for cost-effective long-term storage.

Integration with Azure Services

- **Azure Backup**: Automate file share backups with point-in-time restore.

- **Azure File Sync**: Sync on-premises file servers to Azure File Storage for hybrid cloud caching.

- **Azure Kubernetes Service (AKS)**: Mount SMB/NFS shares to containers for persistent storage.

- **Azure VMs**: Attach file shares as network drives to VMs running Windows or Linux.

Explore Azure Tables

Introduction to Azure Table Storage

Azure Table Storage is a NoSQL data store in the cloud included in the Azure Storage services. It enables you to handle huge amounts of structured, non-relational data in a scalable, cost-effective manner. Azure Table Storage can manage data that is not structured in any required way; therefore, Azure Table Storage doesn't need a fixed schema like that of relational databases. Hence, this makes it a nice choice for a developer who needs flexibility and quick access to data.

It is based on the key-value pair model, where each entity is identified by a partition key and a row key pair. This allows for good querying and operations, in turn, when data is well partitioned.

Key Concepts and Data Model

Further, Azure Table Storage is structured into tables, and each table is a collection of entities. An entity is like a row in a traditional database, and each entity can have as many as 252 individual properties. These properties are name-value and don't have any predefined schema so the data model is quite flexible.

To uniquely identify an entity, you use a combination of a **PartitionKey** and a **RowKey**:

- The **PartitionKey** is used to group related entities together and helps with data distribution and load balancing.

- The **RowKey** is the unique ID for an entity within a given partition.

Together, these keys provide fast lookup and efficient access to data.

Partitioning and Scalability

Azure Table Storage has many important features, and partitioning is one of them. Data is automatically sharded by the PartitionKey, and each shard can be queried independently. It enables you to scale out reads and writes horizontally with your dataset. A partitioned architecture allows for efficiency and can help protect users against throttling.

When to Use Azure Table Storage

Azure Table Storage is excellent for situations between requiring to save a huge volume of structured but streamlined information on a restricted basis as well as a complete relational data resource. It's typically used in cases like

- **IoT and Telemetry Data**: Storing high-speed sensor or device logs

- **Audit Logs and Activity History**: Applications that generate large volumes of logging information

- **User Profile and Session Data**: Apps that store user preferences or session state in a flexible schema

- **Catalogs or Product Inventories**: Storing catalog-style information where items may vary slightly in structure

- **Configuration Data**: Lightweight key-value configuration and reference data that can be read quickly by apps

Accessing Azure Table Storage

You can interact with Azure Tables using various tools and SDKs. These include

- Azure SDKs (available in languages like .NET, Java, Python, Node.js, and more)
- Azure CLI or PowerShell
- Azure Storage REST API
- Azure Storage Explorer (a GUI tool for viewing and managing storage accounts)

Here's a simple example in C# using the Azure SDK:

```
var tableClient = new TableClient(connectionString, "MyTable");
await tableClient.AddEntityAsync(new TableEntity("User", "001")
{
    { "FirstName", "Naveen" },
    { "LastName", "Kumar" }
});
```

Azure Table Storage vs. Azure Cosmos DB Table API

You can also use Azure Cosmos DB by means of the Table API for table storage capabilities. Azure Cosmos DB retains its advantages as an advanced, fully managed database service with global distribution,

CHAPTER 4　EXPLORING NON-RELATIONAL DATA ON AZURE

low-latency reads and writes, automatic indexing, and tunable throughput, even though both services use the same programming model and structure.

How does Azure Cosmos DB work? Azure Cosmos DB is best for applications where you have stringent performance requirements and a user globally distributed. In contrast, Azure Table Storage is more suitable for less advanced scenarios with lower latency and availability requirements.

Azure Cosmos DB: A Multi-model Database Service

Explore Azure Cosmos DB: Key Features and When to Use

Introduction to Azure Cosmos DB

Azure Cosmos DB is Microsoft's fully managed, globally distributed, multi-model NoSQL database service, designed for high availability, low latency, and elastic scalability for mission-critical applications. Azure Cosmos DB enables developers to build global high-performance applications with fast and consistent access to data on a massive scale.

What differentiates Azure Cosmos DB is its ability to natively support multiple data models and corresponding APIs in one service. With Azure Cosmos DB, there's a data model to match, whether your app works with documents, key-value pairs, graphs, or columnar data.

Key Features

1. **Global Distribution**

   - Deploy data to any Azure region worldwide with automatic replication.

   - Multi-region writes enable low-latency access for globally distributed users.

2. **Multi-model and Multi-API Support**

   - Supports document (JSON), key-value, graph, and column-family data models.

   - Compatible with popular APIs like SQL, MongoDB, Cassandra, Gremlin (Apache TinkerPop), and Azure Table Storage.

3. **Elastic Scalability**

   - Independently scale storage and throughput (provisioned or serverless modes).

   - Automatically scales to handle spikes in demand without downtime.

4. **Guaranteed Performance**

   - Single-digit millisecond latency for reads/writes.

   - 99.999% availability SLA for multi-region accounts.

5. **Consistency Flexibility**

   - Five tunable consistency levels (strong, bounded staleness, session, consistent prefix, eventual) to balance performance and data accuracy.

6. **Integrated Analytics**
   - Built-in support for real-time analytics with Azure Synapse Link.

7. **Security and Compliance**
   - Encryption at rest and in transit, private endpoints, and compliance certifications (e.g., GDPR, HIPAA).

8. **Cost Optimization**
   - Serverless mode for sporadic workloads and autoscale for predictable traffic.

When to Use Azure Cosmos DB?

1. **Globally Distributed Applications**
   - Apps requiring low-latency access across continents (e.g., gaming, retail, social platforms)

2. **High-Scale, Low-Latency Workloads**
   - Real-time scenarios like IoT telemetry, fraud detection, or recommendation engines

3. **Multi-model Data Needs**
   - Applications using diverse data types (e.g., JSON documents, graph relationships, or key-value pairs)

4. **Migration from Existing NoSQL Databases**
   - Lift-and-shift MongoDB, Cassandra, or Gremlin-based apps with minimal code changes

5. **Unpredictable or Rapidly Growing Workloads**
   - Startups or enterprises needing elastic scaling without manual intervention

6. **Mission-Critical Systems**

    - Applications requiring 99.999% uptime and robust disaster recovery

7. **Real-Time Analytics**

    - Combine operational and analytical workloads using Synapse Link for near real-time insights

Explore APIs for Azure Cosmos DB

Azure Cosmos DB is a globally distributed, multi-model database for any scale built on Microsoft's planet-scale data infrastructure – an anonymous service natively supporting both relational and non-relational workloads. They can use popular open source database engines like PostgreSQL, MongoDB, and Apache Cassandra to build or migrate applications. When creating the Azure Cosmos DB instance, you are choosing the database engine startup based on data type, existing application compatibility, developer support, etc.

Azure Cosmos DB for NoSQL

Microsoft's native non-relational service designed specifically for the document data model is called Azure Cosmos DB for NoSQL. It saves information as JSON documents with queries written using SQL-like syntax.

Example Query

Retrieve product details from a catalog:

SQL

```
SELECT *
FROM products p
WHERE p.productId = "P101"
```

Result

```
{
   "productId": "P101",
   "name": "Wireless Mouse",
   "price": 29.99,
   "category": "Electronics"
}
```

Azure Cosmos DB for MongoDB

This API is compatible with MongoDB's BSON (Binary JSON) data model, so developers can use MongoDB client libraries and syntax.

Example Query

Find a user by email in the users collection:

JavaScript

```
db.users.find({ email: "alice@contoso.com" })
```

Result

```
{
   "_id": "5f3d8a9e",
   "email": "alice@contoso.com",
   "displayName": "Alice Brown",
   "lastLogin": "2023-10-05T14:23:54Z"
}
```

Azure Cosmos DB for PostgreSQL

This is a scalable PostgreSQL-based distributed relational database. It is also capable of supporting relational tables and SQL queries.

CHAPTER 4 EXPLORING NON-RELATIONAL DATA ON AZURE

Example Table

OderId	Customer	Total
1001	Naveen	149.99
1002	Priya	89.95

Example Query
SQL

```
SELECT Customer, Total
FROM Orders
WHERE OrderID = 1001;
```

Result

Customer	Total
Naveen	149.99

Azure Cosmos DB for Table

This is a key-value store optimized for high scalability, compatible with Azure Table Storage.

Example Table

PartitionKey	RowKey	Item	Stock
Electronics	E123	Headphones	120
Furniture	F456	Dask Lamp	75

127

Example Request
Retrieve the desk lamp stock using the Table API:
Http

```
GET https://endpoint/Inventory(PartitionKey='Furniture',RowK
ey='F456')
```

Azure Cosmos DB for Apache Cassandra

This is a column-family store compatible with Apache Cassandra, allowing flexible schemas.

Example Table

ISBN	Title	Author	Genre
978-978-045152	1984	George Orwell	Dystopian
978-006112	The Alchemist	Paulo Coelho	

Example Query
SQL

```
SELECT * FROM Books WHERE ISBN = '978-045152';
```

Result

ISBN	Title	Author	Genre
978-978-045152	1984	George Orwell	Dystopian

Azure Cosmos DB for Apache Gremlin

It manages graph data with vertices (nodes) and edges (relationships).

Example Graph
A social network graph showing users (vertices) and friendships (edges).

Example Queries

1. Add a new user vertex:

   ```
   g.addV('user').property('userId', 'U4').
   property('name', 'Carlos')
   ```

2. Create a friendship edge:

   ```
   g.V('U4').addE('friendsWith').to(g.V('U2'))
   ```

3. Retrieve users sorted by join date:

   ```
   g.V().hasLabel('user').order().by('joinDate')
   ```

Common Use Cases for Azure Cosmos DB

The Azure Cosmos DB service is a multi-model database service for modern applications offering global distribution, low latency, and high throughput in a single database service. Here, I'm sharing some of the scenarios which Azure Cosmos DB shines.

1. Globally Distributed Applications

Data can be replicated in multiple Azure regions for low-latency access to users worldwide through Azure Cosmos DB's turnkey global distribution.

Example Use Case

- A **social media app** with users in North America, Europe, and Asia stores profiles and posts in Azure Cosmos DB, ensuring fast reads/writes regardless of location.

Key Benefits

- Automatic multi-region replication
- Single-digit millisecond latency
- Configurable consistency levels

2. IoT and Telemetry Data

These capabilities require the use of a scalable data layer that helps organizations deal with the time-series data generated by a large number of IoT devices, sensors, and logs at a high rate and high volume – Azure Cosmos DB is designed to excel at exactly this.

Example Use Case

- A **smart home system** ingests millions of sensor readings (temperature, motion, energy usage) daily. Azure Cosmos DB scales elastically to manage spikes in data ingestion.

Key Benefits

- High write throughput (millions of requests/sec)
- Serverless option for cost-efficient scaling
- Time-to-live (TTL) for automatic data expiration

3. Real-Time Personalization and Recommendations

The low-latency queries provided by Azure Cosmos DB are ideal for real-time recommendation engines.

Example Use Case

- An **ecommerce platform** uses Azure Cosmos DB to store user behavior data (clicks, purchases) and generates personalized product recommendations in milliseconds.

Key Benefits

- Fast reads/writes for dynamic user profiles
- Flexible schema (NoSQL) for evolving data models
- Integration with Azure Synapse for analytics

4. Gaming Leaderboards and Player Data

Gaming applications need high-speed reads/writes for leaderboards, player inventories, and live updates.

Example Use Case

- A **mobile battle royale game** uses Azure Cosmos DB to track real-time player stats, match history, and global rankings with minimal lag.

Key Benefits

- Single-digit millisecond response times
- Automatic scaling during peak gaming hours
- Support for both document (NoSQL) and key-value (Table) models

5. Multi-tenant SaaS Applications

Azure Cosmos DB's partitioning and scalability makes it ideal for SaaS apps that serve so many customers.

Example Use Case

- A **CRM platform** stores customer data for thousands of businesses, with each tenant's data isolated in a logical partition.

Key Benefits

- Efficient partitioning for tenant isolation
- Cost-effective scaling per tenant demand
- Support for relational (PostgreSQL) and NoSQL models

6. Fraud Detection and Financial Transactions

Transactional throughput must be low latency, deterministic, and auditable.

Example Use Case

- A **payment processing system** uses Azure Cosmos DB to log transactions, detect anomalies, and prevent fraud in real time.

Key Benefits

- Strong consistency for financial accuracy
- High availability with 99.999% SLA
- Encryption at rest and in transit

7. Content Management and Catalog Systems

Azure Cosmos DB's flexible schema is great for dynamic content, such as product catalogs or media libraries.

Example Use Case

- A **streaming service** stores movie metadata (genres, actors, ratings) in Azure Cosmos DB, enabling fast searches and personalized content feeds.

Key Benefits

- Schema-agnostic storage (JSON documents)
- Full-text search integration (Azure Cognitive Search)
- Geo-replication for global content delivery

Summary

The evolution of modern applications is leaning toward non-relational data solutions that can comprehensively scale to handle diverse data types. With this chapter, we examined concepts as well as some Azure services used to manage non-relational data.

1. Non-relational vs. Relational Data

The foundation of this chapter contrasted two data paradigms:

- Non-relational (NoSQL) data allows developers to have flexible schemas, ensures horizontal scalability, and is optimized for unstructured/semi-structured data formats such as JSON documents, key-value pairs, and graph data.

- Relational data has to have rigid schemas (tables, rows, and columns), making it powerful for less complex joins and transactions.

2. Azure Storage Services for Non-relational Data

Azure provides specialized services for different non-relational data needs:

- **Azure Blob Storage**: Ideal for unstructured data like images, logs, and backups

- **Azure Data Lake Storage Gen2**: Optimized for big data analytics with hierarchical namespace

- **Microsoft OneLake**: Unified data lake solution within Fabric for all analytics workloads

CHAPTER 4   EXPLORING NON-RELATIONAL DATA ON AZURE

- **Azure File Storage**: Managed file shares accessible from cloud or on-premises
- **Azure Table Storage**: Simple NoSQL key-value storage for lightweight scenarios

3. Azure Cosmos DB: The Multi-model Database Powerhouse

Azure Cosmos DB stands out with its

- **Enterprise-Grade Features**: Global distribution, single-digit millisecond latency, automatic scaling, and 99.999% availability SLA
- Multi-model support through various APIs
  - **NoSQL (Core SQL):** Native JSON document storage
  - **MongoDB**: Fully managed MongoDB-compatible service
  - **Cassandra**: Column-family store for wide-column data
  - **Gremlin**: Graph database for relationship-rich data
  - **Table**: High-scale key-value storage
  - **PostgreSQL**: Distributed relational database capabilities

4. Real-World Applications of Azure Cosmos DB

The chapter highlighted transformative use cases:

- **Global Applications**: Delivering low-latency access across worldwide regions
- **IoT Solutions**: High-velocity ingestion and processing of sensor telemetry
- **Personalization Engines**: Dynamic user profiling and real-time recommendations
- **Gaming Platforms**: Millisecond-response leaderboards and player data
- **SaaS Applications**: Efficient multi-tenant architectures with isolated partitions

This comprehensive exploration of non-relational data solutions on Azure equips you to select optimal storage and database services based on your specific data characteristics, performance requirements, and scalability needs. The next step is to apply this knowledge by experimenting with these services in practical scenarios.

CHAPTER 5

Analytics Workloads on Azure

In this chapter, you will go deep into big data analytics and how to ingest, process, and store that data. You will be introduced to the fundamental differences between batch and streaming data and how these differences influence the analytics workflows. The chapter also delves into Azure analytical data stores, such as Azure Synapse Analytics and Data Lake Storage, and the comparison between data warehouses and data lakes. You'll know what they are, what they do, and how to select the best solution for your analysis requirements.

You will then turn your attention to real-time data analytics, including streaming data analytics, and the tools Azure offers for real-time data processing, including Azure Stream Analytics, Event Hubs, and IoT Hub.

The chapter concludes with Microsoft Power BI for data visualization. You will learn the capabilities Power BI provides for your data discoveries, how to work with the different elements of a data model, and how to properly choose visualizations.

By the end of this chapter, you will have an overview of workloads, analytics, and capturing and analyzing real-time data, as well as gain experience with visualizing data with Power BI items that are necessary when using Azure to do advanced analytics.

CHAPTER 5   ANALYTICS WORKLOADS ON AZURE

Explore Fundamentals of Large-Scale Analytics

Describe Data Warehousing Architecture

Overview

Enterprise data warehousing solutions integrate traditional data warehousing (often behind business intelligence) and big data processing patterns – big data analytics patterns. Conventional DWs generally use data loaded from Online Transaction Processing (OLTP) systems and have a schema optimized for complex queries (analysis) over the data, often in a multidimensional model. By comparison, big data solutions process mountains of disparate data in a variety of formats, as it arrives or in batches, into a data lake. Distributed data processing systems (e.g., Apache Spark) are then employed in analyzing this data. Combining scalable and flexible data lake storage with the powerful structured querying available in data warehouses has resulted in a modern architectural design pattern known as the data lakehouse.

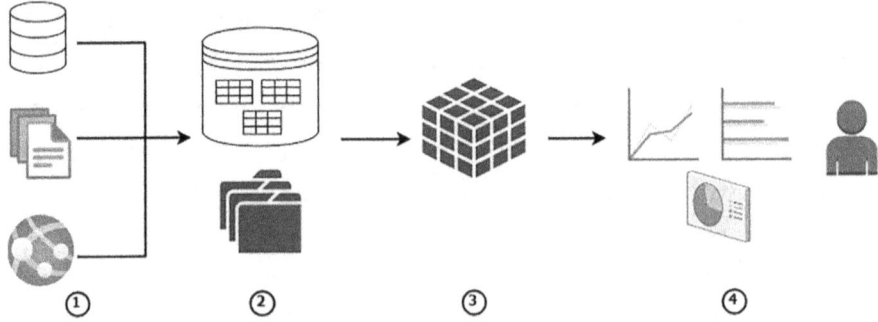

Figure 5-1. Data Warehousing Architecture

CHAPTER 5   ANALYTICS WORKLOADS ON AZURE

Figure 5-1 shows the data warehousing architecture with four major components labeled as 1, 2, 3, and 4. The functions of these components are explained in detail below.

1. Data Ingestion and Processing

At the heart of any analytics workload is data ingestion. Data is ingested from different sources in Azure transactional databases, files, APIs, and real-time streams into a data lake or a relational data warehouse.

This workflow usually adheres to an ETL (Extract, Transform, Load) or ELT (Extract, Load, Transform) pattern:

- **ETL**: Data is cleaned, filtered, and transformed before being loaded into the analytical store.
- **ELT**: Raw data is loaded first and then transformed within the analytical environment.

Both strategies target the preprocessing of data into a structure best suited for analysis and querying.

To handle high volume of data, these are components Azure leans to distributed processing systems such as Apache Spark pools in Azure Synapse, which are multi-node clusters working together to perform parallel processing.

Data ingestion is available for batch processing (processing static data based on a schedule) as well as real-time stream processing for nearly instant insight from live data sources.

2. Analytical Data Store

The aggregated or processed data is stored in an analytical data store (a system built to support large-scale query and analysis). Azure has several such types:

- Relational data warehouses (e.g., Azure Synapse SQL pools)
- File system–based data lakes (e.g., Azure Data Lake Storage Gen2)
- Hybrid solutions, like data lakehouses or lake databases, which combine the features of both for greater flexibility and performance

These stores are designed to support high-speed analytical workloads and can scale with increasing data demands.

3. Analytical Data Model

While data scientists and analysts can query the data in the store directly, it's typical to create analytical models that make reporting more straightforward and faster. These models

- Pre-aggregate data for efficient access
- Support multidimensional analysis using cubes that aggregate metrics (e.g., total sales) across dimensions like time, product, or geography
- Enable drill-up and drill-down navigation to explore data at various levels of detail

Tools like Power BI and Azure Analysis Services are often used to create these models.

4. Data Visualization

Now comes the last step: turning the data into insights. With applications such as Power BI, analysts and even those who are not technically savvy can create reports, dashboards, and visualizations. These visuals

- Highlight trends, comparisons, and key performance indicators (KPIs)
- Can be shared via printed reports, documents, presentations, or interactive web dashboards
- Empower self-service analytics across an organization

Visualization brings the analytical power of the data warehouse to life, enabling data-driven decision-making at all levels.

Explore Data Ingestion Pipelines
Overview

After you learn how big data analytics is built and distributed and the system patterns applied to the processing of massive volumes of data, the next important thing to master is data ingestion: the process of moving data from a variety of sources into a big data store for processing and analysis.

In Azure, data ingestion is generally facilitated via the use of data pipelines, which automate the movement of data from source systems to data lakes or data warehouses. They serve as the backbone for developing scalable, repeatable, and manageable data workflows – especially in enterprise settings with dozens of data sources and complex transformations.

Data Pipelines in Azure

To implement large-scale ingestion pipelines, Azure offers two major services:

- **Azure Data Factory (ADF)**: A fully managed, serverless data integration service that enables the creation, scheduling, and monitoring of ETL/ELT workflows
- **Microsoft Fabric Pipelines**: A newer, unified experience built into Microsoft Fabric, allowing users to manage ingestion, transformation, and storage in a single collaborative environment

Both services provide a visual or code-based interface to define pipelines that automate the movement and transformation of data at scale.

Key Components of Data Ingestion Pipelines

1. Pipeline Structure

A pipeline consists of

- **Activities**: Individual tasks that perform operations (e.g., copying data, running transformations)
- **Datasets**: Represent the input and output data structures (e.g., CSV files, SQL tables)
- **Linked Services**: Define connections to external data sources (e.g., Azure Blob Storage, SQL Database)

2. Types of Activities

Pipelines support different activity types:

- Data movement activities (copy data from source to destination)
- Data transformation activities (apply transformations using Azure Databricks, SQL, or custom code)
- Control flow activities (conditional logic, loops, branching)
- Built-in activities (predefined tasks like web calls or stored procedures)

3. Linked Services and Integration

Linked services connect pipelines to external systems, such as

- Azure Blob Storage/ADLS Gen2 (for raw data ingestion)
- Azure SQL Database/Synapse SQL (for relational transformations)
- Azure Databricks/Spark (for big data processing)
- Azure Functions (for custom logic)

4. Execution and Orchestration

Pipelines can be triggered:

- On a schedule (e.g., daily/hourly batches)
- Event based (e.g., new file arrival in Blob Storage)
- Manually (ad hoc execution)

ETL vs. ELT in Azure Pipelines

Table 5-1 shows a high-level comparison of the two data integration approaches commonly used in Azure.

Table 5-1. ETL vs. ELT in Azure Pipeline

ETL (Extract, Transform, Load)	ELT (Extract, Load, Transform)
Data is transformed before loading into the warehouse	Data is loaded into the warehouse before being transformed
Best for structured data with predefined schemas	Ideal for raw/unstructured data (e.g., data lakes)
Uses Azure Data Factory + Databricks for transformations	Uses Azure Data Factory + Databricks for transformations

Example: Building a Pipeline in Azure Data Factory

1. Ingest Raw Data
   - Use a Copy Activity to pull data from a source (e.g., on-prem SQL Server ➤ Azure Blob Storage).
2. Transform Data
   - Apply a data flow (Spark based) or stored procedure (SQL based) for cleansing.
3. Load into Analytical Store
   - Output to Azure Synapse, Fabric Lakehouse, or Power BI.
4. Monitor and Schedule
   - Set up failure alerts and automated triggers.

CHAPTER 5 ANALYTICS WORKLOADS ON AZURE

Microsoft Fabric Pipelines (Unified Approach)

If using Microsoft Fabric, pipelines integrate seamlessly with

- OneLake (unified data lake storage)
- Warehouses and lakehouses (for structured and semi-structured analytics)
- Power BI (For visualization)

This end-to-end integration simplifies management compared to stand-alone ADF.

Why Use Data Pipelines?

Data pipelines offer numerous benefits in large-scale analytics scenarios:

- **Automation**: Schedule and run ingestion workflows without manual intervention.
- **Scalability**: Handle massive volumes of data from various sources.
- **Modularity**: Separate stages of ingestion, transformation, and loading for better reusability.
- **Monitoring and Logging**: Track pipeline executions, detect failures, and debug issues using built-in monitoring tools.
- **Flexibility**: Combine services and technologies tailored to specific tasks – whether that's a simple copy operation or a complex ML transformation.

CHAPTER 5　ANALYTICS WORKLOADS ON AZURE

Explore Analytical Data Stores

In a modern data analysis environment, Analytics Data Stores plays a distinctive role in allowing organizations to store, manage, and analyze large amounts of data effectively. These stores are designed for rich queries and data exploration, operating at human interactive latencies for users ranging from analysts to data scientists.

There are two types of modes of analytical data stores: the data warehouse and the data lake. On top of that, hybrid solutions, like data lakehouses, are coming up – trying to give you the best from the two worlds.

1. Data Warehouses

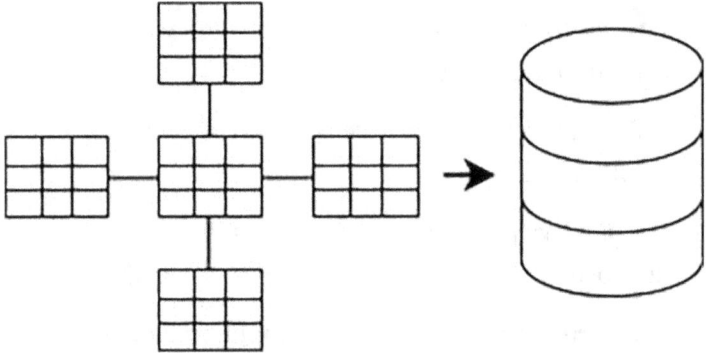

Figure 5-2. Data Warehouse

As shown in Figure 5-2, data warehouses are centralized repositories specifically designed for analytical queries and reporting. They store structured data in a predefined schema and are optimized for fast, SQL-based querying.

CHAPTER 5 ANALYTICS WORKLOADS ON AZURE

Key Characteristics

- Stores highly structured and cleansed data
- Follows a schema-on-write model
- Supports complex queries and aggregations
- Ideal for business intelligence (BI), reporting, and dashboards
- Often uses star or snowflake schemas

Azure Example

- Azure Synapse Analytics (formerly SQL Data Warehouse) is Microsoft's cloud-based data warehouse that integrates enterprise data warehousing with big data analytics.

2. Data Lakes

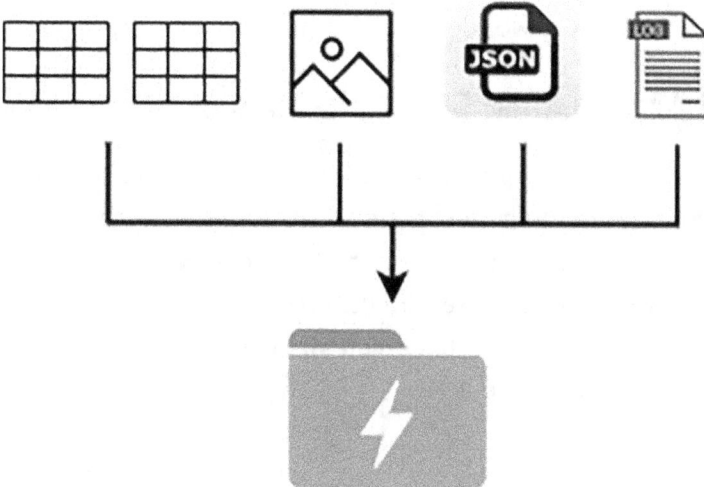

Figure 5-3. Data Lake

As shown in Figure 5-3, data lakes are designed to store vast amounts of raw data – both structured and unstructured – at any scale. They support a schema-on-read approach, which means the data is interpreted and structured at the time of analysis.

Key Characteristics

- Stores raw data in its native format (e.g., JSON, CSV, images, logs)
- Supports structured, semi-structured, and unstructured data
- Ideal for machine learning, big data processing, and real-time analytics
- Provides flexibility for data exploration and experimentation

Azure Example

- Azure Data Lake Storage Gen2 is a highly scalable and secure data lake built on Azure Blob Storage, optimized for analytics workloads.

Hybrid Approaches: Data Lakehouses

To address the challenges associated with using each of these platforms alone, firms are adopting more hybrid "data lakehouse" approaches.

A data lakehouse is an architecture that includes the structure and reliability of a data warehouse with the openness and direct access to data of a data lake. It allows users to execute BI queries directly on raw or semi-structured data with SQL engines.

Key benefits

- Unified storage for structured and unstructured data
- Reduces data movement between lakes and warehouses

CHAPTER 5   ANALYTICS WORKLOADS ON AZURE

- Supports both traditional BI and modern AI/ML workloads

- Allows for real-time analytics with lower latency

Azure Services for Analytical Data Stores

Azure provides powerful services to implement data warehouses, data lakes, and hybrid lakehouse solutions.

Microsoft Fabric

Microsoft Fabric is an end-to-end analytics platform that unifies data engineering, data science, data warehousing, and BI into a single integrated experience.

- Offers lakehouse as a native concept combining data lake and warehouse functionalities

- Built on OneLake, a unified storage layer that serves all Fabric workloads

- Enables seamless collaboration between data engineers, analysts, and scientists

- Includes Power BI, Data Factory, and Synapse experiences for complete analytics workflows

Use Case: Ideal for organizations looking for a cohesive, all-in-one platform with deep integration between ingestion, transformation, modeling, and visualization.

Azure Databricks

Azure Databricks is a collaborative analytics platform built on Apache Spark, optimized for big data and AI workloads.

- Supports large-scale data processing using Spark SQL, Python, Scala, and R
- Integrates well with Azure Data Lake for lakehouse architecture
- Offers Delta Lake, a powerful storage layer that brings ACID transactions to data lakes
- Enables machine learning, data science, and advanced analytics

Use Case: Best suited for scenarios requiring powerful distributed computing, real-time data processing, and advanced machine learning workflows.

Bringing It All Together

In each of these cases, you can consider these services as an analytical data store in that you get a schema and interface through which you can query the data. But in many cases, the data is actually sitting in a data lake, and the service is about processing this data and running queries.

Some options may even link the use of these services. An Extract, Load, and Transform (ELT) ingestion process could copy data into a data lake, followed by using one of these services to transform the data and the other to query it. For instance, a pipeline might use a notebook running in Azure Databricks to munge a very large amount of data in the data lake and then move it into a SQL in Microsoft Fabric Warehouse to perform additional analysis and reporting on the cleansed data.

Explore Fundamentals of Real-Time Analytics

Understand Batch and Stream Processing

Overview

Driven by higher technology adoption by people, businesses, and institutions, in conjunction with the proliferation of smart devices and broad internet access, data generation has exploded. This data is consistently collected from different channels, i.e., IOT sensors, social media, transaction systems, and applications.

A lot of this data can be analyzed in real time (or near real time), allowing systems to offer real-time insights, automatic responses, and event trend discovery as events take place.

This subsection is intended to give a high-level understanding of real-time data processing, how processing can be classified into batch and streaming, and introduce the Azure services that can help you to realize real-time analytics solutions.

What Is Data Processing?

At its core, data processing is the transformation of raw data into structured, meaningful information. This can support decision-making, analytics, and automation.

There are two general types of data processing.

1. Batch Processing

Batch processing involves collecting large volumes of data over time and processing them together in a scheduled or triggered operation.

- **How It Works**: Data is ingested, stored temporarily, and then processed as a group.

- **When It's Used**: Ideal for periodic reporting, historical analysis, and large ETL/ELT workloads.

For example, imagine you want to track the number of likes on your social media posts. A batch processing approach would mean you wait until the end of the day, gather all the likes from every post, and then count them all at once, as shown in Figure 5-4.

Batch Method

- You check your posts only once at midnight.

- You count all the likes that accumulated throughout the day in one go.

- You don't know the exact number of likes until the batch counting is done.

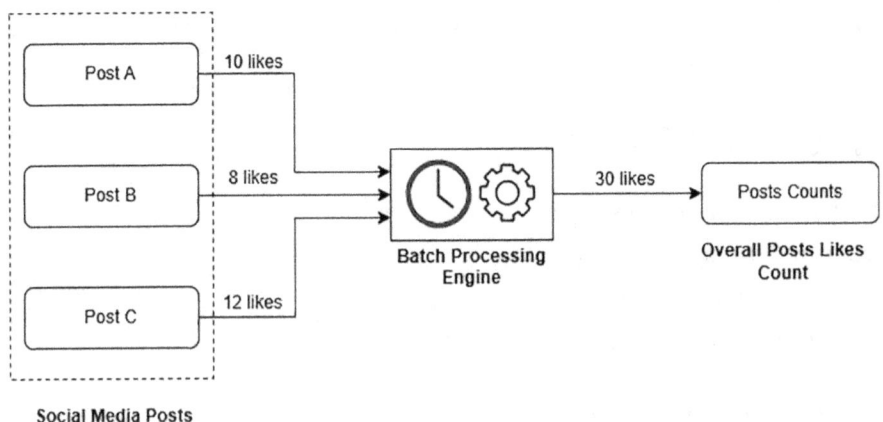

Figure 5-4. Batch Processing Example

CHAPTER 5   ANALYTICS WORKLOADS ON AZURE

Real-World Example

A retail chain collects all sales transactions throughout the day. At midnight, it runs a batch job to calculate daily totals, generate dashboards, and update inventory.

Advantages

- Handles large data volumes efficiently
- Optimized for performance and cost in periodic jobs
- Easier to debug and manage workflows

Disadvantages

- Not suitable for real-time insights.
- Delays in processing may cause outdated results.
- All input data must be ready and validated before processing. Any errors or crashes can stop the entire batch job. Even minor issues may require fixing and rerunning the full job.

Azure Services

- Azure Data Factory
- Azure Synapse Analytics
- Microsoft Fabric (Data Pipelines and Warehouses)

2. Stream Processing

Stream processing involves analyzing data in motion – as soon as it is generated.

- **How It Works:** Each data point is ingested and processed in real time or near real time with minimal delay.

153

CHAPTER 5 ANALYTICS WORKLOADS ON AZURE

- **When It's Used**: Perfect for detecting fraud, monitoring IoT devices, alerting, or personalizing user experiences instantly.

If your post goes viral and gets thousands of likes per hour, waiting until the end of the day means you miss real-time updates. For instance, instead of waiting until midnight to count likes, a streaming approach would track and display each new like the moment it happens, giving you real-time updates, as shown in Figure 5-5.

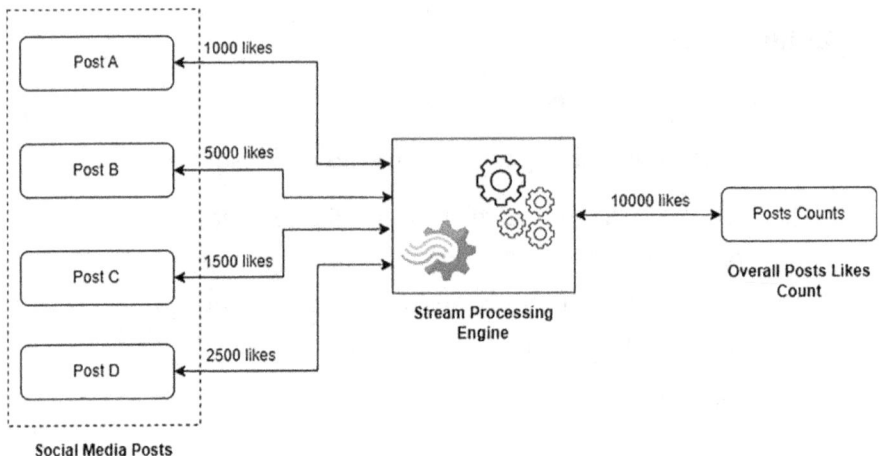

Figure 5-5. Steam Processing Example

Real-World Example

An online food delivery app tracks rider locations in real time and uses stream processing to estimate delivery times and send alerts when food is near the customer.

Advantages

- Enables real-time decisions and alerts
- Immediate visibility into critical operations
- Supports time-sensitive applications (e.g., fraud detection, live dashboards)

CHAPTER 5   ANALYTICS WORKLOADS ON AZURE

Disadvantages

- Complex to design and scale
- Requires robust error handling and latency control

Azure Services

- Azure Stream Analytics
- Azure Event Hubs
- Azure IoT Hub
- Azure Databricks (Structured Streaming)

Batch vs. Stream Processing: Key Differences

While both batch and stream processing transform raw data into actionable insights, they differ significantly in how they handle and analyze data:

- **Data Scope**
    - *Batch processing* works with the entire dataset at once, allowing comprehensive analysis across all available data.
    - *Stream processing* deals with real-time data, typically focusing on recent records or a sliding time window (e.g., the last 30 seconds).
- **Data Size**
    - *Batch processing* efficiently handles large volumes of data collected over time.
    - *Stream processing* is optimized for individual records or small sets of data (micro-batches) as they arrive.

- **Performance (Latency)**
  - *Batch jobs* usually have higher latency, often processing data every few hours or at scheduled intervals.
  - *Stream processing* provides near real-time responsiveness, with latencies measured in seconds or milliseconds.
- **Type of Analysis**
  - *Batch processing* is ideal for in-depth, complex analysis, such as reporting, trend discovery, and historical comparisons.
  - *Stream processing* supports real-time use cases, like live dashboards, alerts, and immediate event-driven actions using simple aggregations or rolling metrics.

Combining Batch and Stream Processing

Most big data analytics systems leverage both batch and stream processing to provide a full perspective (e.g., based on history and live facts).

In classic form, stream processing is used for collecting and processing real-time data (filters or aggregates) and rendering immediate insights via live dashboards (e.g., the number of cars going through a point per hour). The cooked data is then cached for future use.

Meanwhile, batch processing may be using this stored data to carry out more complex, heavy-duty analysis like spotting traffic trends over the last 12 months.

CHAPTER 5 ANALYTICS WORKLOADS ON AZURE

Even if you are not concerned with immediate insights, streaming technologies are still helpful for acquiring and loading real-time data into storage systems. This data can then be processed in batches at a later time, like rounding up cars in a parking lot and then counting them.

A hybrid model is the best for the enterprise for many use cases. It permits businesses to respond to live signals as well as overarching historical trends.

Example Use Case

A smart factory monitors machines in real time using stream processing to detect faults and raise alerts. At the same time, it uses batch processing to analyze production trends, optimize performance, and schedule maintenance.

Benefits of Hybrid Approaches

1. Balance between real-time action and deep analysis
2. Supports both time-critical and strategic use cases
3. Enhances reliability and scalability

Figure 5-6 shows some ways in which batch and stream processing can be combined in a large-scale data analytics architecture.

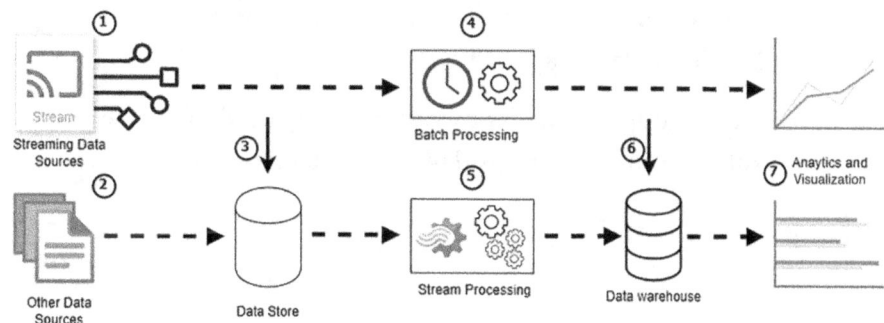

Figure 5-6. *Batch and Stream Processing*

CHAPTER 5 ANALYTICS WORKLOADS ON AZURE

Figure 5-6 illustrates the integration of batch and stream processing within a modern data architecture. The diagram highlights key components involved in this hybrid approach, labeled as 1, 2, 3, and so on. Each of these numbered elements is explained below:

1. Streaming data is captured in real time as events occur.

2. Data from other sources is ingested into a data store – typically a data lake – for batch processing.

3. If immediate analysis isn't needed, real-time data can be stored first and processed later in batches.

4. For real-time analytics, stream processing technologies are used to filter or aggregate incoming data over time windows for instant insights or visualizations.

5. Batch processing is used at intervals to prepare non-streaming data for analysis, with results stored in an analytical data store (often a data warehouse) for long-term insights.

6. Processed results from real-time streams can also be stored in the analytical data store to support combined historical analysis.

7. Visualization and analytics tools are then used to explore both real-time and historical data together.

Core Components of a Stream Processing Architecture

While there are numerous tools and technologies available to build a stream processing solution, most architectures share a set of foundational components, regardless of the specific implementation. Let's explore the typical structure and services that underpin stream processing in Azure.

A High-Level Overview of Stream Processing Architecture

At its core, a basic stream processing architecture typically includes the stages given in Figure 5-7.

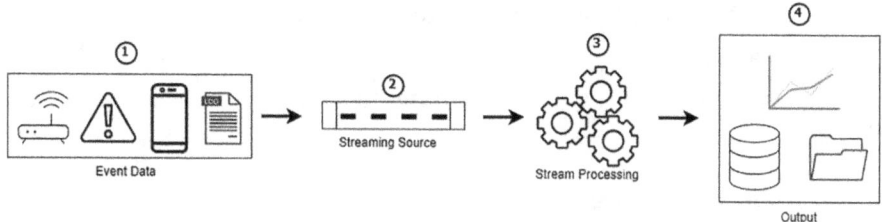

Figure 5-7. Stream Processing Architecture

Figure 5-7 shows the stream processing architecture, with the key components labeled as 1, 2, 3, and 4. Each of these parts is explained in detail below:

1. **Event Generation**

    A data stream starts with an event; an example is the reading of a sensor, the user posting something on social media, or the logging of an entry in a file – anything that generates data in digital form.

2. **Data Ingestion (Streaming Source)**

   A streaming source retrieves the produced data – in simpler systems, perhaps a folder in cloud storage or a table in a database. More mature structures rely on message queues or event hubs to guarantee the orderliness and correctness of one-time data processing so they can provide guaranteed and ordered event transmission.

3. **Stream Processing Logic**

   Processing of incoming data occurs in real time and is accomplished by a long-running query or processing job. This logic could filter out specific event types, project or change data fields, or calculate aggregations over a window of time – such as counting the number of temperature readings we see every minute.

4. **Output Delivery (Sink)**

   The sink is where the stream processing results are sent. This might be a file system, a database table, a real-time dashboard, or another queue for more processing.

Real-Time Analytics Technologies in Azure

To implement real-time stream analytics, Microsoft provides a range of services, including

CHAPTER 5   ANALYTICS WORKLOADS ON AZURE

- **Azure Stream Analytics**

    A fully managed Platform as a Service (PaaS) offering that allows you to create streaming jobs. These jobs ingest data from streaming sources, apply real-time queries, and write the results to various outputs.

- **Spark Structured Streaming**

    A powerful open source library used for building scalable stream processing solutions on Apache Spark. It integrates well with Azure services like Azure Databricks and Microsoft Fabric.

- **Microsoft Fabric**

    An integrated data analytics platform that supports a wide range of data operations, including real-time analytics, data engineering, data science, and more – all within a unified environment.

Data Sources for Stream Processing in Azure

Various Azure services can serve as input sources for stream processing workflows:

- **Azure Event Hubs**

    A highly scalable event ingestion service that handles data streams, ensuring messages are processed in order and exactly once.

- **Azure IoT Hub**

    Tailored for managing data from IoT devices, this service provides a secure and efficient way to stream telemetry data from the edge to the cloud.

- **Azure Data Lake Storage Gen2**

    Though commonly used for batch analytics, this scalable storage solution can also act as a source for stream processing under certain scenarios.

- **Apache Kafka**

    A widely adopted open source event streaming platform often used in combination with Apache Spark for real-time data pipelines.

Output Targets (Sinks) for Stream Processing

Once data has been processed, it is typically routed to one or more of the following sinks:

- **Azure Event Hubs**

    Enables the queuing of processed data for subsequent downstream operations.

- **Azure Data Lake Storage Gen2, Microsoft OneLake, or Azure Blob Storage**

    These services provide persistent storage of processed data in file formats suitable for further analysis or archiving.

- **Azure SQL Database, Azure Databricks, Microsoft Fabric**

    These platforms allow processed data to be stored in relational or distributed tables, making it accessible for querying and advanced analytics.

- **Microsoft Power BI**

    Facilitates real-time data visualization by integrating with streaming datasets, empowering users to build live dashboards and interactive reports.

Explore Microsoft Fabric Real-Time Intelligence

In today's world of data-driven organizations, the desire to work with data as soon as it arrives vs. in retrospect is paramount. Microsoft Fabric Real-Time Intelligence is built for this: it's a platform that lets you ingest, analyze, and react to streaming data at scale. It allows users to unlock the value of data in motion and deliver insights "in the moment" across the organization.

This solution is applicable to most real-time and event-driven use cases – ranging from monitoring events in IoT telemetry, live log streams, etc. By basing decisions, strategies, campaigns, and programs on data gathered in real time – in giant buckets or in small – the real-time intelligence capability allows organizations to be nimble, confident, and right every time.

Key Features of Real-Time Intelligence in Microsoft Fabric

1. End-to-End Streaming Solution

Real-time intelligence is a complete pipeline to consume, process, analyze, and visualize data in real time. It covers all steps, from data input to data output and everything in between, without the need for users to write too much code.

2. Unified Real-Time Hub

This capability is powered by the Real-Time Hub – an organization-wide stream data catalog and data platform. It removes the barriers of time-sensitive data discovery, sharing, and integration among departments. This single landscape means everybody has current info, which promotes not just strong decision-making but also cooperation.

3. No-Code Data Connectivity

Microsoft Fabric makes stream processing systems easier to develop with a no-code library of connectors. These connectors allow rapid connection to any number of streaming sources, which can include internal systems, third-party services, IoT devices, and more, with no need for custom development.

4. Rich Visualizations and Dashboards

Users can interactively explore patterns, discover anomalies, and forecast trends with intuitive dashboards after data is ingested and processed with Real-Time Intelligence. Developers can simply drop these dashboards into their workflows, and they can take advantage of them to apply natural language queries, AI-powered assistants like Copilot, and drag-and-drop interfaces meant to make insights accessible to even non-technical users.

5. Real-Time Alerts with Reflex

Use Reflex – a feature that enables you to create alerts and automatic responses to conditions to act upon insights. For instance, when sensor information is found to be abnormal, a service ticket or an email alert can be issued on the spot, which can be used not only for the control of the situation, such as abnormal situations in other operation facilities, but also for the rapid management of a business-critical event.

CHAPTER 5   ANALYTICS WORKLOADS ON AZURE

6. Geospatial and Advanced Analytics

Real-Time Intelligence enables geospatial analysis, which is great for applications involving physical locations – like tracking vehicles, monitoring assets, or enacting logistics based on the weather. Paired with real-time predictions and machine learning models, it makes for smart analysis well beyond basic KPIs.

Exploring and Acting on Data in Real Time

Working with Real-Time Intelligence typically begins with selecting a live data stream – either from within the organization or an external partner. Once selected, the platform provides robust tools to

- Visualize key metrics and trends
- Identify unexpected spikes, drops, or outliers
- Forecast future values using real-time models
- Share insights across teams using dashboards and alerts

From exploration to action, every component is designed to minimize latency and maximize business value.

How Real-Time Intelligence Fits into Microsoft Fabric

One of the greatest strengths of Real-Time Intelligence is its **deep integration with the wider Microsoft Fabric ecosystem**, including

- **Data Factory** for data movement and transformation
- **Data Engineering** for scalable processing
- **Data Science** for advanced modeling

- **Power BI** for visualization and reporting
- **OneLake** for unified data storage

This alignment ensures that real-time and batch data processing coexist in a cohesive, secure, and scalable environment.

Explore Apache Spark Structured Streaming

In the current life of big data, such organizations have to handle huge streams of data in a continuously incoming manner. Apache Spark, a powerful distributed processing engine, provides an idiomatic SIMD-like API for arbitrary expression trees to be executed over location-transparent static and streaming datasets. In Microsoft Azure, such as Microsoft Fabric and Azure Databricks, Spark acts as a powerful data processing platform, and it is also used for advanced analytics.

Apache Spark: A Unified Engine for Batch and Streaming

Apache Spark is intended to execute applications in parallel across a cluster, which is a great basis for processing large datasets. It is usable with several programming languages, like Python, Scala, Java, etc., and has a wide variety of usage, from ETL and machine learning to real-time analytics.

One important feature of Spark is its integrated processing framework, which provides a unified platform and codebase for batch and stream processing, simplifying system building effectively.

Introducing Spark Structured Streaming

Spark Structured Streaming has many methods to do stream processing that have set coarse boundaries between batch and interactive queries, but Structured Streaming continues the trend from Spark's first release (0.8) of blurring these boundaries.

Real-time data stream processing is provided by using Apache Spark and the Spark Structured Streaming library. This high-level streaming API makes it easy to consume, process, and analyze real-time data streams in Apache Spark using dataframe and SQL-like semantics.

How It Works

- **Ingestion**: Data is continuously read from a streaming source (e.g., Apache Kafka, cloud file stores, or network sockets) into an **unbounded dataframe** – a Spark structure that grows as new data arrives.

- **Transformation**: You define a query on this dataframe to **filter**, **project**, or **aggregate** the streaming data. Often, these operations are applied over **time-based windows** to derive meaningful trends (e.g., average sensor readings per 10-minute interval).

- **Output**: The results of the query generate a new dataframe, which can be directed to various sinks such as databases, cloud storage, or real-time dashboards.

This abstraction allows developers to think about streaming data in the same way as static data – making real-time processing more accessible and easier to maintain.

Use Cases for Spark Structured Streaming

Spark Structured Streaming is well suited for use cases that require

- Real-time ingestion into data lakes or warehouses
- Continuous monitoring and alerting based on event data

CHAPTER 5   ANALYTICS WORKLOADS ON AZURE

- Joining and enriching live data streams with historical records
- Scalable streaming pipelines integrated with batch workloads

Its compatibility with the broader Spark ecosystem ensures seamless integration with machine learning libraries, SQL engines, and big data storage formats.

Delta Lake: Enhancing Stream and Batch Consistency

To further strengthen Spark's capabilities, Microsoft Azure supports **Delta Lake** – an open source storage layer that brings **reliability, consistency, and schema enforcement** to data lake architectures.

With Delta Lake, you can

- Ensure **ACID-compliant** transactions on streaming data
- Apply **schema validation** to enforce data quality
- Use a **single table** for both batch and stream processing
- Enable **time travel** queries for point-in-time data analysis

Delta Lake seamlessly integrates with Spark Structured Streaming, allowing tables to act as both streaming **sources** and **sinks**. For example, you could ingest streaming log data into a Delta table, perform windowed aggregations, and write the results back to another Delta table for dashboard reporting.

Spark on Microsoft Azure: Where It All Comes Together

Both **Microsoft Fabric** and **Azure Databricks** provide managed Spark environments that natively support Structured Streaming and Delta Lake. These platforms offer

- Auto-scaling compute clusters
- Built-in data connectors and monitoring tools
- Integration with Power BI for real-time visualization
- Support for collaborative development in notebooks and pipelines

Whether you're building a real-time recommendation engine, monitoring IoT sensors, or processing financial transactions as they happen, Spark Structured Streaming combined with Delta Lake offers a **scalable and resilient** foundation for streaming analytics in Azure.

Explore Fundamentals of Data Visualization with Microsoft Power BI

Introduction

In this data-driven world, you don't just collect and store data. The power of data is actually unlocked when it's converted into great insights. And here you need the wonders that data visualization can do for you. Data visualization is the graphical representation of information and data. It facilitates the understanding of complex concepts, recognizing patterns, and discovering trends faster and more efficiently.

In this chapter, we will discuss what I consider to be the basics of data visualization in Microsoft Azure. The tool at the top of our list of business analytics tools is Microsoft Power BI, one of the most powerful and popular tools in the same category.

Capabilities and Features of Power BI

What Is Power BI?

Power BI is a suite of business analytics tools to analyze data and share insights. Monitor your business and get answers quickly with rich dashboards available on every device. It is an interactive visualization and business intelligence tool that provides an interface where end users can create their own reports and dashboards.

Key Components of Power BI

Power BI comprises several components that work together in a streamlined workflow.

1. Power BI Desktop

- A free Windows desktop application used for creating reports and data visualizations
- Allows users to connect to multiple data sources, transform the data using Power Query, and create robust data models
- Primary development tool for building Power BI reports

2. Power BI Service (Power BI Online)

- A cloud-based service (SaaS) where users publish, share, and collaborate on reports
- Allows dashboard creation and access to reports from anywhere
- Includes features like scheduled data refresh, row-level security, and workspace collaboration

3. Power BI Mobile Apps

- Native apps for iOS, Android, and Windows devices
- Enables users to access and interact with their reports and dashboards on the go

4. Power BI Report Server

- An on-premises solution for hosting Power BI reports behind your firewall
- Useful for organizations with strict data governance or compliance requirements

5. Power BI Gateway

- Bridges on-premises data sources and the Power BI cloud service
- Enables scheduled refresh and live queries against on-prem data sources

Power BI Workflow: From Data to Dashboard

Understanding the typical Power BI workflow helps in mastering its use for analytics and visualization. The process generally involves the following steps.

Step 1: Connect to Data Sources

Power BI supports a wide range of data sources, including

- Excel and CSV files
- Azure SQL Database and SQL Server

- Azure Data Lake and Blob Storage
- Online services like Microsoft 365, Dynamics 365, Salesforce, and more

Step 2: Transform and Clean Data

Using Power Query Editor, users can

- Clean data (remove duplicates, handle missing values)
- Filter, sort, and merge data
- Rename columns and change data types
- Create calculated columns and measures

Step 3: Model the Data

Data modeling involves defining relationships between tables and optimizing the data structure for analytics. Key tasks include

- Creating relationships using foreign keys
- Using DAX (Data Analysis Expressions) to add calculated columns, measures, and KPIs
- Organizing tables into star schemas where possible

Step 4: Create Visualizations

Users can drag and drop fields onto the report canvas to build

- Bar, line, and pie charts
- Maps and geographical visuals
- Tables and matrix visuals
- Slicers and filters for interactive exploration

Step 5: Publish and Share

Once the report is ready

- Publish it to the Power BI Service
- Create and pin visuals to dashboards
- Share reports and dashboards with stakeholders
- Set up data refresh schedules and alerts

Step 6: Collaborate and Act

Through integration with Microsoft Teams, SharePoint, and Power Platform, users can

- Collaborate on reports
- Automate workflows using Power Automate
- Embed reports in apps or web portals

Benefits of Using Power BI for Data Visualization

- **Ease of Use**: Intuitive drag-and-drop interface suitable for beginners and advanced users alike
- **Scalability**: Handles datasets from small Excel files to large-scale enterprise data warehouses
- **Real-Time Dashboards**: Supports live dashboards with real-time streaming data
- **Advanced Analytics**: Integration with Python, R, and AI capabilities for deeper analysis
- **Security**: Supports role-based access, row-level security, and compliance with global standards

Building Data Models in Power BI

As businesses become more data driven, how that data is organized becomes more and more important. Data modeling is a fundamental aspect of analytics through which you can arrange data in logical structures to enable effective querying and insightful analysis. A good data model will help to increase your performance, simplify your reporting, and drive a level of consistency in your analytics.

Understanding Analytical Models

Analytical models offer a structured way to organize such data to facilitate thoughtful analysis. Such models are usually based on sets of related data in which there are both measurable values and descriptive attributes.

At the heart of an analytical model are two key elements:

- **Measures**: These are numeric values you want to analyze, such as sales, profit, or units sold.
- **Dimensions**: These are the descriptive entities that provide context for measures – like products, customers, or time periods.

Think of an analytical model as a multidimensional grid – commonly referred to as a cube – where each cell in the grid represents an aggregated measure for a unique combination of dimension values. For example, this structure allows you to answer questions such as

- What is the total revenue per product category?
- How many items were sold each month?
- Which customer segment contributed most to total sales?

By organizing data in this manner, analytical models enable fast, intuitive exploration of trends and performance metrics across different business perspectives.

Tables and Schema Design

Dimension Tables

Dimension tables contain information about the items you might use to categorize or filter data. A separate row in a dimension table is a distinct, individual entity instance of that type of object (one time for each product, each customer, etc.), and all of the descriptive characteristics about that object are in that row.

For instance, a product dimension table could have the following columns:

- ProductID (unique identifier)
- ProductName
- Category
- Brand

Similarly, a customer dimension may contain

- CustomerID
- FullName
- City
- Region

Dimension tables act as the filters and groupings in your analysis, so they are crucial in giving your model context to the raw data.

It's also typical to add a Date or Time dimension to see any trends of the data over time (e.g., by year, quarter, or month).

Fact Tables

Fact tables contain quantitative data the measures being analyzed. Each row in a fact table represents a fact or an event and is linked to dimension tables, i.e., it contains the respective foreign keys.

For a Sales fact table, one can have

- SaleID
- DateKey
- ProductKey
- CustomerKey
- QuantitySold
- Revenue

This structure allows you to summarize numerical values on related dimensions – think sum total revenue by product or average purchase value by customer.

As fact tables tend to be high in row count, they are optimized for read operations and aggregation.

Attribute Hierarchies

In practice, it is common for analysts to seek data from a variety of levels of detail. Here is where that relates to attribute hierarchies: hierarchies enable cut mechanisms so that users can drill down from a broad view to more specified contexts – and roll up for an overview.

Some examples of attribute hierarchies are

- **Time Hierarchy**: Year ➤ Quarter ➤ Month ➤ Day
- **Product Hierarchy**: Category ➤ Subcategory ➤ Product Name
- **Geographic Hierarchy**: Country ➤ State ➤ City

In the presence of hierarchies, a lightweight analytical model makes dynamic and user-friendly exploration possible. For instance, a sales report could first display aggregate sales by year that can be clicked to drill into monthly or even daily sales.

Hierarchies also support calculations that are pre-aggregated at every level, improving the speed and usability of analysis.

Data Modeling in Microsoft Power BI

Microsoft Power BI provides a powerful environment for building data models for analysis. From Model view in Power BI Desktop, you can

- **Define Relationships**: Create relations links between the fact table and the dimension table by creating one-to-many relationships on keys.

- **Set Data Types**: Confirm fields are set with the correct data types – money for revenue and dates for date/time data.

- **Create Hierarchies**: Categorize fields and create drillable levels to help users navigate between similar fields in reports.

- **Manage Table Properties**: Handle what fields are displayed and how they're formatted, summarized, or sorted.

- **Build Calculated Columns and Measures**: Write formulas in DAX (Data Analysis Expressions) and include summary values in your model, such as profit margins or year-over-year growth.

By building a strong model in Power BI, you are able to provide your visualizations with a firm, performant, and scalable substrate. The modeling layer serves as a unified source of truth, ensuring various reports and dashboards share the same metrics and definitions.

Choosing the Right Visualization for Insights

After you have that well-trained data model, the next step in the analytics is creating charts. Visualizations make raw data beautiful and easy to navigate and act upon. The "right" visualization type is important for effective communication of insights and enabling data-driven decision-making.

Key Considerations for Data Visualization

Before getting into the nitty-gritty of visual design, it's useful to know the fundamental rules that underpin effective data visualization.

1. Know Your Audience

Various stakeholders need different layers or insights. And one executive might want the big picture, whereas an analyst may want all the nitty-gritty detail. Make visualizations that are audience appropriate and level of data literacy appropriate.

2. Select the Right Visualization Type

All charts were not created equal. The data type and the story you want to tell should influence your selection of visualization. For instance, line charts are more appropriate for displaying trends over time, while comparisons among categories are better shown using bar or column charts.

3. Prioritize Clarity and Simplicity

Avoid cluttered visuals. A clean, bold design allows your audience to viscerally comprehend your insights. Make sure to use readable color palettes, axis labels, and legends.

4. Ensure Accuracy

I mean, visualizations need to be representative of the data. Misrepresentative scales, flawed aggregations, or cut-off axes can mislead and result in wrong decisions.

5. Use Interactivity Wisely

Interactive capabilities let users interrogate the data the way they want – filtering, drilling, or highlighting aspects of a report. But interactivity should enhance the story you are telling, not muddy it.

Common Visualization Types in Power BI

Power BI includes a large set of built-in visuals, which can be further extended by custom visuals available in the AppSource marketplace. Some of the frequently used visual types are listed below.

1. Tables and Text Cards

We can use these cases to illustrate which parts of the system exhibit good performance when given a particular input. Tables showing the raw figures for a trend provide a structured representation of the raw figures when a comparative distinction is to be drawn or when displaying hundreds or even thousands of related measurements.

Cards provide multiple types of single values (e.g., totals, averages, or KPIs) and highlight important values (e.g., total revenue or count of customers).

Use Case: If you have a bunch of sales numbers, you would like to display them and quickly see the profit or revenue.

2. Bar and Column Charts

These charts are perfect to compare quantities of categories. With the exception of orientation (they are horizontal or vertical, respectively), the two chart types are identical in structure.

Use Case: When you want to compare the revenue by product category or by customer segment across various regions.

3. Line Charts

Line charts are also a good choice for displaying trends over time. They're really great for seeing patterns, seasonality, and performance evolution.

Use Case: IF-THEN conditions on monthly sales growth or website traffic over weeks.

4. Pie and Donut Charts

The charts present data in proportions or percentages, and they essentially make up fractions of a circle as well over here. Though they're attractive, they do serve as an obstruction – particularly for numerous categories, you should only use them as a special effect.

Use Case: Show the market share of various product lines.

CHAPTER 5 ANALYTICS WORKLOADS ON AZURE

5. Scatter Plots

Scatter plots display the relationship between two numeric variables. They can be used to detect correlations, clusters, or outliers in the data.

Use Case: Let's say we want to analyze if there is a relationship between how much money we spend on marketing and how that influences the amount of revenue that is coming in.

6. Maps

Maps chart data that have a geographic element to them. Power BI has different map visuals you can use (filled maps, background images, shape maps, and map visualizations, including bubble maps) to view geographic data on the map.

Use Case: Compare sales between stores or track shipping per region.

Interactive Reports in Power BI

One of the beautiful things about Power BI is the built-in capability to create interactive reports. In these reports

- Value from one visual can filter or cross-highlight other visuals.
- Users can add slicers to filter data throughout the report by date, product, region, and other factors.
- At the very least, as end users drill down to higher levels of detail, they would like to investigate that data at higher levels of dumps (year to quarter to month).

For example, when a user clicks "Seattle" in a column chart showing sales by city, all of the other visuals in the report change to only show metrics related to Seattle.

181

CHAPTER 5 ANALYTICS WORKLOADS ON AZURE

This interactivity transforms a static dashboard into a dynamic, self-service analytics feature in which users can explore data as they see fit.

Summary

In this chapter, you learned the basics of analytics workloads on Microsoft Azure and how cloud technologies can help you analyze data on a massive scale, gain real-time analytics, and create visuals to intuitively explore data. The chapter consisted of three major sections.

1. Explore Fundamentals of Large-Scale Analytics

Data analysis at scale is particularly critical for data-driven decision-making by today's enterprises. This section has introduced fundamental ideas about data warehousing and ingestion pipelines and the analytic data stores that are used to facilitate high-volume, high-performance analytics workloads.

- **Data Warehousing Architecture**: You learned how data warehouses, including Azure Synapse Analytics, can bring structured data into a unified analytical store. The design decouples computation from storage, which makes this architecture scalable, massively parallelized, and performance enhanced.

- **Data Ingestion Pipelines**: Pipelines to ingest data is the process of importing data from different sources into an analytical system. You learned about Azure Data Factory and Azure Synapse Pipelines – tools that can be used to efficiently orchestrate, transform, and load data from a variety of sources.

- **Analytics Data Stores**: You considered Azure-native data stores such as Azure Data Lake Storage and Azure Synapse Dedicated SQL Pools, which can handle petabyte-scale datasets for storage and querying. These systems are designed for fast read operations, and they serve as the analytical query engine for data engineers and analysts.

2. Explore Fundamentals of Real-Time Data Analytics

This section drilled into real-time insights with Azure, which does this by processing data as it arrives – an absolute must for some applications, such as fraud detection, live dashboards, and IoT telemetry.

- **Batch vs. Stream Processing**: You learned the distinction between batch (processing big sets of data at once) and stream processing (processing data as it arrives) and when you might prefer one over the other.

- **Stream Processing Architecture Basics**: While not listed in the original frameworks, the key pieces of a modern real-time pipeline from event ingestion (Event Hubs or IoT Hub), processing engines (Azure Stream Analytics or Apache Spark Structured Streaming), and output sinks (Power BI or big data stores) were covered.

- **Microsoft Fabric Real-Time Intelligence**: This upcoming solution provides a converged platform for streaming data ingestion, processing, and visualization, using familiar and easy-to-scale tools. It accelerates time to insight with its rich integration with the Microsoft data stack.

CHAPTER 5   ANALYTICS WORKLOADS ON AZURE

- **Apache Spark Structured Streaming**: You saw how Spark gives you scalable, distributed stream processing, making it easy to do complex transformations, joins, and aggregations in near real time on your real-time data feeds using well-known API types.

3. Explore Fundamentals of Data Visualization with Microsoft Power BI

The last section stressed the need for data to be transformed into visual understanding for business and the democratization of analytics.

- **Power BI Capabilities and Features**: Power BI has strong data modeling, transforming, and visualization capabilities. You got exposure to main elements like Power BI Desktop, Power BI Service, and mobile apps and how it integrates with Excel and Azure services.

- **Creating Data Models in Power BI**: Data models are the backbone of analysis. You learned how Power BI allows you to preprocess data to build analytical models, such as tables from tables (fact and dimension tables) and hierarchies, and how we can use DAX to create calculated measures and columns.

- **Selecting the Appropriate Visualization for Insights**: How good your report is depends on how you use the visual. You examined common kinds of visualizations, such as tables, bar and line charts, maps, and scatter plots, and discovered how Power BI creates filterable reports where users can interact with their data.

CHAPTER 6

Exam Preparation and Practice

Overview

You have made your way through the world of Azure data services, ranging from core database concepts to cloud-native data tools, and now comes the most exciting part – let's put it all together! This is the final chapter that will walk you through how to prepare for the exam, as well as the exam objectives, and help assess if you are ready to pass the Microsoft DP-900: Azure Data Fundamentals certification exam.

Online vs. Offline Exam Readiness

Depending on your preference and availability, Microsoft offers two delivery modes for the DP-900 exam:

- **Online (Remote Proctored)**
- **Offline (Test Center Based)**

Each has specific requirements. Here's how to prepare for both.

CHAPTER 6   EXAM PREPARATION AND PRACTICE

Online Exam Readiness (Remote Proctored Exam)

Taking the exam from home or office is convenient but comes with strict technical and environmental requirements.

A. System and Technical Requirements

- A **reliable PC** or **Mac** with
  - Windows 10 or later/macOS 10.13 or later
  - Google Chrome or Microsoft Edge browser
  - Webcam (internal or external)
  - Microphone
- **Stable internet connection** (minimum 1 Mbps upload/download)
- Install the **OnVUE software** from Pearson VUE system check: HYPERLINK "https://www.microsoft.com/en-us/learning/online-exams.aspx"

Tip   Run the system test **at least two days before** your exam to detect hardware, software, or firewall issues.

B. Environment Readiness

- Room must be
  - Well lit
  - Quiet and free of disturbances

CHAPTER 6   EXAM PREPARATION AND PRACTICE

- No unauthorized materials (books, phones, notepads)
- Desk/table must be **clear** – no external monitors, sticky notes, or headphones.
- You'll be asked to use your **webcam to scan the room** before the exam starts.
- **No breaks allowed** unless specified (accommodations must be pre-approved).

C. ID Verification

- Valid **government-issued photo ID** (name must match your Microsoft account exactly).

D. Best Practices

- Log in **30 minutes early**.
- Close all applications and background processes.
- Follow proctor instructions strictly – violations may result in test termination.

Offline Exam Readiness (Test Center–Based Exam)

If you prefer a controlled environment and better focus, you can take your exam at an authorized **Pearson VUE test center**.

CHAPTER 6   EXAM PREPARATION AND PRACTICE

A. Booking a Test Center

- Find a nearby test center.
- Choose your time slot and location, and receive a confirmation email.

B. What to Bring

- Valid **government-issued ID** with a photo and signature
- Confirmation email (optional but helpful)

Note   Some centers require **two forms of ID**, so read your appointment instructions carefully.

C. What to Expect

- Your items (phone, bag, etc.) will be stored in a locker.
- You'll go through a **security check**, including photo and palm scan (in some locations).
- An administrator will guide you to your workstation.
- Scratch paper or erasable whiteboards may be provided for notes.

D. Center Etiquette

- Arrive **15–30 minutes early**.
- Maintain silence and follow all proctor instructions.
- Breaks are typically allowed but **pause the exam timer**.

CHAPTER 6   EXAM PREPARATION AND PRACTICE

Tip   Choose a test center with good reviews and low noise levels.

Exam Tips and Common Pitfalls

Successfully passing the DP-900 exam not only requires understanding the content but also being aware of how to approach the questions effectively. Here are some practical tips to help you prepare.

General Tips

- **Read the Question Carefully**: Many questions include qualifiers like "not," "best," or "most appropriate." These words can change the entire meaning of the question.

- **Don't Rush**: Take your time to review all answer options before selecting one, especially when multiple answers may be correct.

- **Eliminate Wrong Answers**: If you're unsure, start by eliminating obviously incorrect options. This improves your odds even when guessing.

Multiple Choice Questions

- Watch out for "all of the above" or "none of the above" options – make sure every statement is true or false before choosing.

- Be cautious of distractors – options that sound correct but don't apply to the specific scenario given.

Drag-and-Drop Questions

- Focus on understanding relationships and sequences. Practice matching services to scenarios and arranging steps logically.

- Double-check the placement before submitting – misplaced items could lead to incorrect answers.

Case Study Questions

- Read the scenario thoroughly before jumping to questions. Understanding the business need or technical environment is key.

- Apply your knowledge contextually; focus on what's best for the scenario, not just what is technically possible.

- Don't bring in outside assumptions. Stick strictly to the information provided.

Common Pitfalls to Avoid

- Overthinking simple questions. If it seems straightforward, it probably is.

- Ignoring instructions. For example, selecting more than one answer when only one is required.

- Not reviewing flagged questions. Always leave time at the end to review any flagged or uncertain responses.

Final Preparation Checklist

- Microsoft Learn modules completed
- Hands-on practice with Azure free services
- At least two full-length practice exams taken
- Technical setup and room environment checked (if online)
- Valid ID ready
- Appointment confirmed and calendar reminder set
- Ready to stay calm, focused, and confident

After the Exam

- You'll receive your score immediately after submitting.
- If you pass, your certification will be available on your Microsoft Learn profile.
- If not, review your performance report and reattempt after 24 hours (retake policy applies).

Practice Questions and Answers

Practice Questions with Explanations

Section 1: Introduction to Data Representation

1. **Which of the following is an example of structured data?**

    A. Log files

    B. JSON documents

    C. SQL tables

    D. Audio recordings

    Answer: C

    Explanation: Structured data is highly organized and easily searchable using simple queries. SQL tables have a defined schema, with data stored in rows and columns, making them the classic example of structured data.

2. **What type of data is best represented in a JSON format?**

    A. Relational data with fixed schemas

    B. Tabular data

    C. Semi-structured data

    D. Binary data

    Answer: C

CHAPTER 6   EXAM PREPARATION AND PRACTICE

Explanation: JSON is a text-based format that supports nested structures and flexible schemas, which makes it suitable for representing semi-structured data, such as logs or configuration files.

3. **Which scenario is best suited for using unstructured data?**

    A. Financial transactions stored in SQL tables

    B. Ecommerce product catalogs

    C. Analyzing images in a computer vision system

    D. Storing product prices in a CSV file

    Answer: C

    Explanation: Images are a classic example of unstructured data because they do not follow a predefined model and require specialized processing and storage.

4. **Semi-structured data typically includes**

    A. Tables with strict schemas

    B. Images and videos

    C. Logs and sensor data in JSON format

    D. Encrypted files

    Answer: C

    Explanation: Semi-structured data like JSON-encoded sensor logs has a loose structure but is not as rigid as relational tables, allowing more flexibility.

CHAPTER 6 EXAM PREPARATION AND PRACTICE

5. **Which of the following is NOT a characteristic of structured data?**

   A. Defined schema

   B. Stored in relational databases

   C. High flexibility in schema design

   D. Uses rows and columns

   Answer: C

   Explanation: Structured data relies on a predefined and rigid schema, which means it is not flexible. Schema changes can be complex and impact data integrity.

Section 2: Data Storage Options

1. **Which of the following file formats is optimized for analytical workloads due to its columnar storage?**

   A. CSV

   B. JSON

   C. Parquet

   D. TXT

   Answer: C

   Explanation: Apache Parquet is a columnar storage format that is highly efficient for queries in analytical workloads because it reads only the required columns.

CHAPTER 6   EXAM PREPARATION AND PRACTICE

2. **What is the key disadvantage of using CSV files for storing large datasets?**

    A. Lack of support for structured data

    B. Inability to be compressed

    C. Inefficient performance with large datasets

    D. No support in Azure services

    Answer: C

    Explanation: CSV files are plain text and do not support columnar storage, compression, or metadata, making them less efficient for processing large datasets.

3. **Which format is best suited for semi-structured data?**

    A. Parquet

    B. CSV

    C. JSON

    D. SQL

    Answer: C

    Explanation: JSON is ideal for semi-structured data because it allows nested and varying attributes across records.

4. **Parquet is particularly effective for which of the following use cases?**

    A. Real-time audio processing

    B. Transactional systems

C. Big data analytics and column-based queries

D. Text-based logging

Answer: C

Explanation: Parquet is optimized for read-heavy analytical queries that process large volumes of data, especially in big data tools like Spark.

5. **Which file format stores data in a human-readable format?**

    A. JSON

    B. Parquet

    C. Avro

    D. ORC

    Answer: A

    Explanation: JSON is a text-based, human-readable format, unlike Parquet or Avro, which are binary formats.

Section 3: Explore Databases

1. **A relational database stores data in**

    A. Key-value pairs

    B. Graph nodes

    C. Tables with rows and columns

    D. Blobs

CHAPTER 6   EXAM PREPARATION AND PRACTICE

Answer: C

Explanation: Relational databases organize data into tables with clearly defined columns (schema) and rows, supporting SQL-based queries.

2. **Which database type is best suited for storing product catalog data with dynamic attributes?**

    A. Relational database

    B. Document database

    C. Column-family database

    D. Time-series database

Answer: B

Explanation: Document databases like MongoDB are ideal for semi-structured data that may vary in structure from document to document, such as product catalogs.

3. **Which is a key feature of non-relational databases?**

    A. Fixed schema

    B. Support for SQL

    C. Schema flexibility

    D. Complex joins

Answer: C

Explanation: Non-relational databases allow flexible schema design, enabling changes to data structure without the need to alter a fixed schema.

197

CHAPTER 6   EXAM PREPARATION AND PRACTICE

4. **Which scenario is ideal for a relational database?**

    A. Real-time telemetry data

    B. User profile data with frequent changes in structure

    C. Financial transaction records

    D. Product reviews with star ratings and comments

    Answer: C

    Explanation: Financial systems require strict data consistency, relationships, and support for ACID transactions, which are best provided by relational databases.

5. **Which of the following is a non-relational database type?**

    A. SQL Server

    B. PostgreSQL

    C. MongoDB

    D. MySQL

    Answer: C

    Explanation: MongoDB is a document-oriented NoSQL database that stores data in BSON format, suitable for semi-structured and unstructured data.

Section 4: Data Workloads

1. **Transactional workloads typically involve**

    A. Complex aggregations over large datasets

    B. Batch processing of historical data

CHAPTER 6 EXAM PREPARATION AND PRACTICE

    C. High volume of real-time transactions

    D. Dashboard visualization

Answer: C

Explanation: Transactional workloads focus on high-throughput, real-time processing of data with ACID compliance, such as order processing systems.

2. **Which is a characteristic of analytical workloads?**

    A. Real-time write performance

    B. High-frequency updates

    C. Large-scale aggregations

    D. Point lookups

Answer: C

Explanation: Analytical workloads often involve summarizing and aggregating large datasets to extract insights, typically in a data warehouse.

3. **Which of the following best differentiates analytical from transactional workloads?**

    A. Analytical workloads are optimized for large-scale reads.

    B. Transactional workloads involve fewer users.

    C. Analytical workloads have strict consistency requirements.

    D. Transactional workloads run infrequently.

Answer: A

Explanation: Analytical systems are tuned for large, read-heavy queries that analyze large datasets, whereas transactional systems are optimized for frequent writes.

4. **Which workload type is best suited for a data warehouse?**

    A. Transactional

    B. Analytical

    C. Real time

    D. Operational

   Answer: B

   Explanation: Data warehouses are designed to support analytical workloads, with optimized storage and query performance for data analysis.

5. **Transactional systems are typically optimized for**

    A. High concurrency and fast writes

    B. Predictive analytics

    C. Dashboarding and BI

    D. Data archival

   Answer: A

   Explanation: Transactional systems handle numerous concurrent users and operations, such as inserts and updates, ensuring fast, reliable transactions.

CHAPTER 6   EXAM PREPARATION AND PRACTICE

Section 5: Roles and Responsibilities in Data Workloads

1. **Which of the following is a key responsibility of a Data Engineer?**

    A. Creating visual dashboards

    B. Managing database access

    C. Designing data transformation pipelines

    D. Writing ad hoc reports

    Answer: C

    Explanation: Data engineers build and maintain pipelines that ingest, transform, and load data for analytics and operational uses.

2. **A Data Analyst primarily focuses on**

    A. Building pipelines for data ingestion

    B. Managing storage infrastructure

    C. Analyzing and visualizing data

    D. Writing stored procedures

    Answer: C

    Explanation: Data analysts derive insights from data through reports, dashboards, and visualizations using tools like Power BI.

CHAPTER 6   EXAM PREPARATION AND PRACTICE

3. **Who is responsible for the availability and performance of a database system?**

   A. Data Analyst

   B. Software Developer

   C. Database Administrator

   D. Data Engineer

   Answer: C

   Explanation: DBAs ensure that databases run efficiently, are secure, and have proper backup and recovery mechanisms in place.

4. **What is a common task of a Database Administrator (DBA)?**

   A. Designing Power BI dashboards

   B. Writing machine learning models

   C. Implementing database backup and recovery

   D. Creating ETL pipelines

   Answer: C

   Explanation: DBAs manage administrative tasks such as backups, maintenance, tuning, and security of the database systems.

5. **Which role is most likely to use Power BI daily?**

   A. Database Administrator

   B. Data Analyst

   C. Data Engineer

   D. Network Engineer

CHAPTER 6   EXAM PREPARATION AND PRACTICE

Answer: B

Explanation: Data analysts frequently use Power BI to create dashboards and share insights with stakeholders.

Scenario-Based Practice Questions
Chapter 2: Understanding Core Data Concepts

Scenario Question:

XYZ Insurance is building a modern data platform on Azure. They manage structured customer data in a SQL database, store semi-structured policy forms in JSON format, and analyze unstructured call center audio recordings. Their team needs to choose optimal file formats for storing this data in Azure, set up both transactional and analytical systems, and assign roles to data professionals across the solution. The business also wants to understand which Azure data services are most appropriate for each part of their workload.

Which of the following combinations BEST supports XYZ's requirements?

    A. Use Azure Data Lake with Parquet for structured data, Cosmos DB for all storage types, implement OLTP workloads for analytics, and have data engineers focus on database indexing.

    B. Use Azure SQL Database for structured data, Blob Storage with JSON for semi-structured data, Data Lake with unstructured audio files, Parquet for analytics, and assign roles: DBAs manage Azure SQL, Data Engineers manage data pipelines, Data Analysts build Power BI dashboards.

203

C. Use Azure Cosmos DB for structured and unstructured data, store everything in CSV format, implement batch workloads for transactions, and assign all tasks to DBAs.

D. Store all data in Azure Table Storage, use only CSV as the file format, define an OLAP system for transactional workloads, and rely solely on Data Analysts for pipeline design.

Correct Answer: B
Explanation:

- Azure SQL is best for **structured data**.
- **JSON files in Blob Storage** are ideal for **semi-structured data**.
- **Azure Data Lake** can handle **unstructured audio files** efficiently.
- **Parquet** is optimal for analytical queries on large data.
- **Transactional and analytical workloads** should be split appropriately.
- **DBAs manage databases, data engineers build pipelines**, and **analysts create insights**, which matches real-world responsibilities.
- Azure provides all the required services.

Chapter 3: Working with Relational Data on Azure

Scenario Question:

ABC Retail wants to migrate their on-premises inventory management system to Azure. Their current database is highly normalized and uses stored procedures and triggers. They are evaluating Azure SQL services

CHAPTER 6 EXAM PREPARATION AND PRACTICE

and also considering open source databases due to their existing PostgreSQL expertise. The team is exploring whether to deploy via a managed service or VMs and want to understand how the choice will affect performance, cost, and manageability.

Which of the following options BEST meets ABC's needs for flexibility, minimal management overhead, and use of existing PostgreSQL skills?

- A. Deploy SQL Server on Azure VMs, manage normalization manually, and run all procedures using T-SQL exclusively.
- B. Choose Azure SQL Managed Instance for all workloads, even those based on PostgreSQL, to centralize administration.
- C. Use Azure Database for PostgreSQL as a fully managed service, continue using normalized schemas and stored procedures, and benefit from minimal management overhead.
- D. Use Azure SQL Database serverless with denormalized data, rewrite PostgreSQL scripts in T-SQL, and manage indexing manually.

Correct Answer: C
Explanation:

- **Azure Database for PostgreSQL** is a **fully managed service** for PostgreSQL users.
- It supports **stored procedures, normalization**, and other advanced features with **minimal overhead**.
- This respects their team's current skillset while taking advantage of Azure's **PaaS capabilities**.

- VM-based deployments would increase management complexity, and switching to SQL Server unnecessarily changes technologies.

Chapter 4: Exploring Non-relational Data on Azure

Scenario Question:

A startup called NKTech is developing a video analysis platform. They store high-resolution videos, log files, and IoT sensor data. The data must be queried flexibly based on attributes (e.g., timestamp, device ID). The team is considering using Cosmos DB to enable global data availability and is exploring which Azure Storage services are most suitable for storing large, unstructured files, with options to scale.

Which solution BEST fits NKTech's needs for storage, query flexibility, and global availability?

A. Use Azure Table Storage for videos and logs and Azure SQL for sensor data; replicate manually across regions.

B. Store videos in Azure Blob Storage, use Cosmos DB with a SQL API for logs and sensor data, and enable global distribution.

C. Use Azure Data Lake Gen2 for all data types and access it through REST APIs for querying IoT data.

D. Use Microsoft OneLake for videos and Cosmos DB with the Gremlin API for querying sensor metrics by timestamp.

CHAPTER 6   EXAM PREPARATION AND PRACTICE

Correct Answer: B
Explanation:

- **Blob Storage** is ideal for **large unstructured data** like video files.

- **Cosmos DB with SQL API** supports **flexible queries** on semi-structured data like logs and IoT readings.

- Cosmos DB's **multi-region replication** and **low latency** features meet the global availability requirement.

- Table Storage and OneLake don't support the rich query capabilities needed here.

Chapter 5: Analytics Workloads on Azure

Scenario Question:

A financial services company is building a real-time analytics dashboard to monitor fraud across global transactions. Data is ingested from multiple sources, including batch data from legacy systems and real-time feeds from APIs. The team uses Microsoft Fabric for real-time processing and wants to design appropriate pipelines and data models. They also need to visualize the data in Power BI to provide timely insights to decision-makers.

Which architecture best meets their goals for ingestion, real-time analytics, and visualization?

A. Use Azure Synapse Pipelines for real-time feeds, store results in a SQL Server VM, and connect to Power BI using imported datasets.

B. Use Azure Data Factory for ingestion, store data in Azure SQL, process with T-SQL scripts, and embed static dashboards in Power BI.

C. Use Microsoft Fabric Real-Time Intelligence for streaming ingestion, Apache Spark Structured Streaming for transformation, store results in a Lakehouse, and use Power BI Direct Lake mode for dynamic visualization.

D. Use Power BI for both ingestion and storage, and create dashboards based on manually uploaded Excel files.

Correct Answer: C
Explanation:

- **Microsoft Fabric Real-Time Intelligence** enables **real-time ingestion**.

- **Apache Spark Structured Streaming** can process data in real time.

- A **Lakehouse** offers scalable storage with analytics capabilities.

- **Power BI Direct Lake** provides **fast, near real-time** insights by directly querying the Lakehouse data without importing.

Mock Exam
Full-Length Practice Test

1. Which of the following best describes semi-structured data?

    A. Data stored in relational tables with fixed schemas

    B. Binary data without any structure

CHAPTER 6   EXAM PREPARATION AND PRACTICE

  C. Data that contains tags or markers to separate data elements

  D. Data stored as plain text files

2. In which scenario is the use of Parquet format most beneficial?

  A. Streaming data ingestion

  B. Low-latency transactional processing

  C. Complex analytical queries with large datasets

  D. Real-time dashboard updates

3. Which statement correctly differentiates between analytical and transactional workloads?

  A. Analytical workloads modify data; transactional ones read data only

  B. Transactional workloads support batch processing

  C. Analytical workloads handle complex queries over historical data

  D. Transactional workloads are not time-sensitive

4. Which role is most responsible for building ETL pipelines and maintaining data flow orchestration?

  A. Data Analyst

  B. Data Engineer

  C. Business Analyst

  D. Database Administrator

5. JSON, CSV, and Parquet are examples of

    A. Database types

    B. Data query languages

    C. File formats for storing structured and semi-structured data

    D. Cloud storage solutions

6. What is a primary advantage of using managed relational databases on Azure?

    A. Full control over OS and hardware configurations

    B. Automatic patching and scaling

    C. Manual tuning of all query plans

    D. Ability to run NoSQL queries

7. Which of the following statements is true about Azure SQL Managed Instance?

    A. It supports only T-SQL and not stored procedures.

    B. It's a fully platform-as-a-service (PaaS) offering with near 100% compatibility with SQL Server.

    C. It's only available in Azure Government clouds.

    D. It is a serverless database only used for dev/test.

8. What does normalization in relational databases primarily aim to achieve?

    A. Maximize disk usage

    B. Increase redundancy for better performance

    C. Eliminate data redundancy and improve data integrity

    D. Speed up transaction commits

CHAPTER 6   EXAM PREPARATION AND PRACTICE

9. Which database object is responsible for ensuring referential integrity?

    A. View

    B. Index

    C. Foreign Key

    D. Trigger

10. Which Azure service would be ideal for hosting a PostgreSQL database with minimal administrative overhead?

    A. Azure Blob Storage

    B. Azure Cosmos DB

    C. Azure Database for PostgreSQL – Flexible Server

    D. Azure SQL Database

11. In what scenario is a NoSQL database like Azure Cosmos DB preferred?

    A. Applications with fixed schemas

    B. OLAP-based data warehouses

    C. Applications requiring high availability and low latency globally

    D. Banking applications with ACID transaction requirements

12. Azure Data Lake Storage Gen2 is optimized for

    A. Low-latency transactional data

    B. Real-time dashboards

    C. Big data analytics with hierarchical namespace support

    D. Mobile app caching

CHAPTER 6   EXAM PREPARATION AND PRACTICE

13. Which Azure service would be most appropriate to store petabytes of unstructured log data for analytics?

    A. Azure File Storage

    B. Azure SQL Database

    C. Azure Blob Storage

    D. Azure Table Storage

14. Which of the following APIs is NOT supported by Azure Cosmos DB?

    A. SQL

    B. MongoDB

    C. Cassandra

    D. MySQL

15. What's a key feature of Microsoft OneLake in Microsoft Fabric?

    A. Only supports structured data

    B. Requires external data warehouse integration

    C. Provides a single unified data lake for all analytics workloads

    D. Built only for use with SQL Server

16. Which service is designed to handle both structured and unstructured data using a multi-model approach?

    A. Azure SQL Managed Instance

    B. Azure Cosmos DB

CHAPTER 6   EXAM PREPARATION AND PRACTICE

   C. Azure Data Factory

   D. Azure Data Explorer

17. A data workload requiring high transactional throughput with strict consistency would benefit most from

   A. Azure Table Storage

   B. Azure Blob Storage

   C. Azure SQL Database

   D. Microsoft Fabric Real-Time Intelligence

18. Which Azure service provides real-time analytics on data streams?

   A. Azure Data Lake Storage Gen2

   B. Azure Blob Storage

   C. Microsoft Fabric Real-Time Intelligence

   D. Azure File Storage

19. What is the role of a foreign key in a relational database?

   A. Improves read performance

   B. Links data between tables and enforces relationships

   C. Allows table partitioning

   D. Tracks historical changes

CHAPTER 6   EXAM PREPARATION AND PRACTICE

20. Which Azure data service supports the Cassandra API?

   A. Azure SQL Database

   B. Azure Table Storage

   C. Azure Cosmos DB

   D. Azure Database for PostgreSQL

21. Which component is crucial in a stream processing architecture?

   A. File storage

   B. Queue or messaging system

   C. Data warehouse

   D. Static ETL jobs

22. Which Azure Storage service provides SMB protocol access?

   A. Azure Table Storage

   B. Azure Blob Storage

   C. Azure File Storage

   D. Azure Data Lake Storage Gen2

23. What is the key benefit of Apache Spark structured streaming?

   A. One-time batch ingestion

   B. Stateless data processing

   C. Real-time processing with fault tolerance and event-time processing

   D. Support only for SQL syntax

CHAPTER 6   EXAM PREPARATION AND PRACTICE

24. Power BI allows users to create data models primarily for

    A. High-performance OLTP systems

    B. Predictive analytics model training

    C. Generating business insights via visualizations

    D. Code-first application development

25. Which type of workload would most benefit from using Azure Synapse Analytics?

    A. A payroll system

    B. A blogging platform

    C. A real-time chat app

    D. A business intelligence system analyzing large datasets

26. Which feature of Power BI allows aggregation of large datasets across multiple data sources?

    A. Power Automate

    B. Power Query

    C. Composite Models

    D. DAX Measures

27. What is a significant difference between a relational and non-relational database?

    A. Relational databases can't be used in cloud environments.

    B. Non-relational databases use fixed schemas.

    C. Relational databases use tabular structures; non-relational databases are more flexible.

    D. Non-relational databases do not support transactions.

28. What is the main advantage of data normalization?

    A. Slower join operations

    B. Better disk utilization through redundancy

    C. Efficient updates by eliminating data duplication

    D. Storing blobs as text

29. Azure Blob Storage is most suitable for

    A. Hosting relational databases

    B. Storing transaction logs

    C. Serving image and video files for a website

    D. Managing SQL stored procedures

30. In Power BI, which feature would you use to perform row-level security?

    A. Data Gateway

    B. DAX Filters

    C. Role Definitions

    D. Visual-Level Filters

31. Which type of database is best for storing IoT sensor data in a time-series format?

    A. Azure SQL Database

    B. Azure Cosmos DB

    C. Azure Table Storage

    D. Azure Data Lake Storage

CHAPTER 6   EXAM PREPARATION AND PRACTICE

32. Which Power BI component helps build dashboards using existing datasets?

    A. Power Query

    B. Power BI Service

    C. Power Pivot

    D. Power Automate

33. What's the role of a Database Administrator in an organization?

    A. Defining visualization logic

    B. Managing and securing database environments

    C. Developing web interfaces

    D. Analyzing market trends

34. Cosmos DB ensures high availability through

    A. Single-node replication

    B. Manual backups

    C. Multi-region replication and consistency models

    D. Infrequent indexing

35. Which feature allows Power BI users to define reusable calculations?

    A. Power Query

    B. Power Apps

    C. DAX

    D. SQL Studio

CHAPTER 6   EXAM PREPARATION AND PRACTICE

36. Which SQL feature allows users to fetch only certain rows meeting specific conditions?

    A. GROUP BY

    B. SELECT *

    C. WHERE clause

    D. JOIN

37. Which Azure service allows scalable ingestion and orchestration of data from multiple sources?

    A. Azure Stream Analytics

    B. Azure Data Factory

    C. Azure Cosmos DB

    D. Power BI

38. One advantage of managed open source databases on Azure is

    A. Complete isolation from cloud environment

    B. No support for backup

    C. High availability with less manual maintenance

    D. Support for Microsoft Access

39. What defines the OLTP workload?

    A. Historical data mining

    B. Real-time analytical dashboards

    C. High-volume read-write operations with short transactions

    D. Massive batch processing

CHAPTER 6   EXAM PREPARATION AND PRACTICE

40. Which Microsoft tool enables near real-time reporting through dashboards?

    A. SSIS

    B. Power Automate

    C. Power BI

    D. Excel Macros

41. Which is not a feature of Azure SQL Database?

    A. Elastic scaling

    B. In-memory processing

    C. Data replication

    D. Hadoop integration

42. What format is columnar and optimized for big data analytics?

    A. CSV

    B. JSON

    C. Parquet

    D. TXT

43. Which capability is offered by Microsoft Fabric Real-Time Intelligence?

    A. Database mirroring

    B. Real-time alerting and analytics using streaming data

    C. Static reporting

    D. SQL Server clustering

CHAPTER 6   EXAM PREPARATION AND PRACTICE

44. Data Analysts primarily use which tool for reporting?

    A. Azure Synapse

    B. Azure Data Factory

    C. Power BI

    D. Azure Data Lake

45. Which Power BI capability allows for custom visual creation?

    A. DAX Editor

    B. Query Editor

    C. Developer Tools and Custom Visual SDK

    D. Dashboard Designer

46. Which Azure service is designed for serverless event processing?

    A. Azure Functions

    B. Azure Table Storage

    C. Azure SQL Database

    D. Azure Active Directory

47. What is a key business benefit of using Azure SQL Database?

    A. Complex manual configurations

    B. Auto-scaling and built-in high availability

    C. Limited data size

    D. No geographic replication

CHAPTER 6   EXAM PREPARATION AND PRACTICE

48. Which type of key helps prevent duplication in a relational table?

    A. Composite Key

    B. Unique Key

    C. Foreign Key

    D. Surrogate Key

49. Which tool allows drag-and-drop visual report creation?

    A. SQL Server Management Studio

    B. Azure Monitor

    C. Power BI Desktop

    D. Visual Studio Code

50. Microsoft Fabric is best described as

    A. A data replication service

    B. A unified platform for data integration, engineering, and real-time analytics

    C. A NoSQL engine

    D. A backup-only solution

Answers and Explanations

1. C – Tags like in XML or JSON structure semi-structured data.

2. C – Parquet is optimized for large-scale analytical queries.

CHAPTER 6   EXAM PREPARATION AND PRACTICE

3. C – Analytical workloads are for large, complex queries over historical data.
4. B – Data Engineers manage pipelines and transformations.
5. C – These are file formats for structured/semi-structured data.
6. B – Managed services reduce overhead with automation.
7. B – SQL MI is a PaaS offering with broad SQL Server compatibility.
8. C – Normalization minimizes redundancy, ensuring data integrity.
9. C – Foreign keys maintain referential integrity.
10. C – Flexible Server offers managed PostgreSQL hosting.
11. C – Cosmos DB supports global distribution and low latency.
12. C – Optimized for big data analytics with Hadoop-compatible storage.
13. C – Blob Storage handles massive unstructured data best.
14. D – Cosmos DB does not support MySQL API.
15. C – OneLake unifies analytics storage in Microsoft Fabric.
16. B – Cosmos DB supports multiple models like key-value, graph, etc.

CHAPTER 6   EXAM PREPARATION AND PRACTICE

17. C – SQL DB is ideal for transactional consistency.
18. C – Microsoft Fabric Real-Time Intelligence supports streaming data analytics.
19. B – Foreign keys enforce relational links between tables.
20. C – Cosmos DB supports the Cassandra API.
21. B – Messaging systems enable real-time data flow.
22. C – Azure File Storage uses SMB protocol.
23. C – Structured streaming is fault-tolerant and supports real-time logic.
24. C – Power BI turns models into business insights.
25. D – Synapse Analytics suits large-scale analytical workloads.
26. C – Composite models integrate datasets across sources.
27. C – Relational uses rigid tables; non-relational is schema-flexible.
28. C – Normalization optimizes update performance by eliminating redundancy.
29. C – Blob Storage handles web file delivery well.
30. C – Role-based row-level security controls access.
31. B – Cosmos DB is well suited for time-series IoT data.
32. B – Power BI Service builds dashboards from datasets.

CHAPTER 6   EXAM PREPARATION AND PRACTICE

33. B – DBAs manage and secure database infrastructure.
34. C – Multi-region and consistency options ensure uptime.
35. C – DAX allows for custom, reusable calculations.
36. C – WHERE limits results based on condition.
37. B – Azure Data Factory integrates and orchestrates data.
38. C – Managed services reduce overhead and increase reliability.
39. C – OLTP involves many quick, read-write interactions.
40. C – Power BI supports real-time dashboarding.
41. D – Hadoop integration is not a native feature.
42. C – Parquet is a columnar format suited to big data.
43. B – Real-Time Intelligence supports alerts and fast queries.
44. C – Analysts use Power BI for visuals and reporting.
45. C – Developers use SDKs to create custom visuals.
46. A – Azure Functions handle serverless event-based logic.
47. B – Built-in scaling and HA are major benefits.
48. B – Unique keys enforce value uniqueness.

CHAPTER 6   EXAM PREPARATION AND PRACTICE

49. C – Power BI Desktop supports drag-and-drop reporting.

50. B – Microsoft Fabric provides an all-in-one analytics platform.

Conclusion

The DP-900 is not just an exam – it's your **first step into the world of cloud data**. Whether you're transitioning careers, validating knowledge, or stepping into a data-related role, this certification lays the foundation.

Go forward confidently. You're more ready than you think. Go get certified!

Index

A

Analytical workloads, 19, 44–47
Apache Avro, 37, 38
Apache Hadoop, 38
Apache Hive, 38
Apache Kafka, 162, 167
Apache Spark, 38, 138, 166
Automation, 51, 145
Azure Blob Storage, 103, 133
    access tiers, 106
    append blobs, 105
    block blobs, 104
    page blobs, 104, 105
    real-world use cases, 106, 107
    three access tiers, 105
Azure Cosmos DB, 54, 102, 121, 122, 125
    for Apache Cassandra, 128
    for Apache Gremlin, 128, 129
    content management and catalog systems, 132
    enterprise-grade features, 134
    features, 123, 124
    fraud detection and financial transactions, 132
    gaming leaderboards and player data, 131
    globally distributed applications, 124, 129
    IoT and telemetry data, 130
    mission-critical systems, 125
    for MongoDB, 126
    multi-model data needs, 124
    multi-model support, 134
    multi-tenant SaaS applications, 131
    for NoSQL, 125
    for PostgreSQL, 126
    real-time personalization and recommendations, 130
    real-time scenarios, 124
    real-world applications, 135
    for Table, 127
Azure Databricks, 9, 55, 111, 150
Azure Data Explorer, 56
Azure Data Factory (ADF), 55, 142
Azure Data Lake Storage Gen2 (ADLS Gen2), 107, 108, 133
    ADF, 111
    vs. Azure Blob Storage, 109
    and Azure Databricks, 111
    and Azure Purview, 111
    and Azure Synapse Analytics, 111

INDEX

Azure Data Lake Storage Gen2 (ADLS Gen2) (*cont.*)
    cost efficiency, 109
    enterprise data lake, 110
    hierarchical namespace, 108
    key features, 108
    log and event analytics, 110
    machine learning pipelines, 110
    optimized for analytics, 108
    real-time analytics, 110
    security, 109
Azure File Storage, 115, 134
    backup and archival, 118, 119
    collaborative development environments, 118
    features, 115
    Lift-and-Shift Linux Workloads (NFS), 118
    network file sharing protocol, 116
    NFS, 116
    protocols for file sharing, 115, 116
    SMB, 116
    storage account tiers, 116–118
Azure OLTP services, 44–46
Azure open source database services, 90, 91
    benefits of Azure Database
        for MariaDB, 92, 93
        for MySQL, 92
        for PostgreSQL, 93
    for MariaDB, 91
    for MySQL, 91
    for PostgreSQL, 91
Azure Relational Data Services
    Azure SQL Database, 81, 83
    Azure SQL Managed Instance, 81, 83
    business benefits
        Azure SQL Database Benefits, 84–86
        comparisons, 87, 88
        SQL Server on Azure VMs Benefits, 86, 87
    comparison, Azure SQL Services, 82
    SQL Server, 81, 84
Azure SQL, 53, 56, 57
Azure Storage, 54, 119
Azure stream analytics, 56, 161
Azure Table Storage, 54, 119, 120, 134
    vs. Azure Cosmos DB Table API, 121, 122
    interact with Azure Tables tools and SDKs, 121
    key-value pair model, 119
    partitioning and scalability, 120
    PartitionKey, 120
    RowKey, 120

B

Binary Large Object (BLOB), 36–37, 103
BSON (Binary JSON), 41, 101, 198

INDEX

C

Charts
　bar, 180
　column, 180
　donut, 180
　line, 180
　pie, 180
Cloud-based storage solutions, 29, 58
Cloud technologies, 182

D

Data analysis, 20, 52, 182
Database management systems (DBMS), 21, 70
Databases, 39, 196–198
　non-relational, 39, 41
　relational databases, 39, 40
Databricks, 55, 150
Data Control Language (DCL), 75
Data Definition Language (DDL), 72–73
Data ingestion, 139, 141
Data lakehouse, 55, 138, 148–149
Data Manipulation Language (DML), 72, 74
Data modeling, 172, 174, 177, 178
Data models
　analytical models, 140, 174, 175
　attribute hierarchies, 176
　creation, 184
　dimension tables, 175
　fact tables, 176

Data pipelines, 142, 145
Data processing
　batch processing, 151
　　advantages, 153
　　Azure services, 153
　　batch method, 152
　　disadvantages, 153
　　example, 152
　　vs. stream processing, 155, 156, 183
　definition, 151
　hybrid approaches, 156–158
　stream processing, 153, 183
　　advantages, 154
　　architecture, 159, 160
　　Azure services, 155
　　data sources, 161
　　disadvantages, 155
　　example, 154
　　output targets, 162
　　real-time stream analytics, 160, 161
Data Query Language (DQL), 73–74
Data representation, 192–194
Data services in Azure
　assets, 52
　Azure Cosmos DB, 54
　Azure Databricks, 55
　Azure Data Explorer, 56
　Azure Data Factory, 55
　Azure SQL, 53
　Azure Storage, 54
　Azure Stream Analytics, 56

229

INDEX

Data services in Azure (*cont.*)
    Microsoft Fabric, 55
    Microsoft Purview, 56
    open source relational
        databases, 53, 54
    roles and services, 56, 57
Data sources, 47, 161–162, 171–172
Data storage
    BLOB, 36
    cloud storage, 29
    CSV file example, 31
    delimited text files, 30
    file format, 30
    JSON, 32, 33
    key characteristics, 30, 31
    optimized file formats, 37–39
    pipe-separated file example, 32
    TSV file example, 31
    XML, 34, 35
Data storage options, 29–30,
    58, 194–196
Data tokens, 20
Data visualization, 141, 169
    considerations, 178, 179
    Power BI, 173
    types, 184
        bar charts, 180
        column charts, 180
        donut charts, 180
        line charts, 180
        maps, 181
        pie charts, 180
        scatter plots, 181
        tables and text cards, 180
Data warehousing (DWs), 138
    architecture, 139, 182
    databricks, 150
    data ingestion pipelines,
        139, 182
        Azure, 142
        benefits, 145
        components, 142, 143
        creation, 144
        ETL *vs.* ELT, 144
        Microsoft Fabric, 145
        overview, 141
    data store, 140, 183
        Azure services, 149, 150
        data lakes, 140, 148
        hybrid solutions, 140, 148
        relational DWs, 140, 146
    ELT, 150
Data workload roles, 49
    Data Analyst, 51, 52
    Database Administrator
        (DBA), 50
    Data Engineer, 50, 51
Data workloads, 41, 198–202
    analytical reporting, 41
    long-term storage and
        retrieval, 41
    OLAP (*see* Online Analytical
        Processing (OLAP))
    OLTP (*see* Online Transaction
        Processing (OLTP))
    real-time transactions, 41

INDEX

transactional *vs.* analytical
workloads, 48, 49
types, 42
Delimited text files, 30, 58
Document Type Definition
(DTD), 35
DP-900 certification, 225
benefits, 4–6, 16
domains and weightage,
6, 16, 17
analytics workloads on
azure, 9, 10
core data concepts, 7
non-relational data,
azure, 8, 9
relational data, azure, 8
flow, 3, 4
professionals, 3, 16
purpose, 2, 3
question types, 10, 11, 17
resources, 14, 15
scoring system, 12, 17
study plan and strategies, 18
analytics workloads on
azure, 14
core data concepts, 12
four-week preparation
plan, 12
non-relational data on azure
(*see* Non-relational data
on azure)
relational data on azure (*see*
Relational data on azure)
time allocation, 12, 17

E, F, G

employees.csv, 31
Exam preparation and practice
case study questions, 190
checklist, 191
common pitfalls, 190
drag-and-drop questions, 190
multiple choice questions, 189
offline exam readiness
center etiquette, 188
expect, 188
requirements, 188
test center, 188
online exam readiness, 186
best practices, 187
environment readiness, 186
ID verification, 187
requirements, 186
practice questions with
explanations
database, 196–198
data representation, 192–194
data storage options, 194–196
data workloads, 198–202
review, 191
scenario-based questions
analytics workloads on
Azure, 207, 208
core data concepts, 203, 204
non-relational data on
Azure, 206, 207
relational data on Azure,
204, 205
tips, 189

231

INDEX

Extensible Markup Language (XML), 34, 35
Extract, Load, Transform (ELT), 139, 150
Extract, Transform, Load (ETL), 139

H, I

Hierarchies, 176–177, 184

J, K, L

JavaScript Object Notation (JSON), 32
JSON data, 24, 25
JSON data structure, 33

M

MariaDB, 51, 71, 89, 90
Microsoft Fabric, 55, 149, 161
Microsoft Fabric Real-Time Intelligence, 163, 183
   data, exploring/action, 165
   end-to-end streaming solution, 163
   geospatial analysis, 165
   integration, 165
   no-code data connectivity, 164
   real-time alerts, reflex, 164
   Real-Time Hub, 164
   visualizations and dashboards, 164

Microsoft OneLake, 111, 133
   See also OneLake)
Microsoft Purview, 56, 111
Microsoft SQL Server, 39, 71
Mock exam
   answers and explanations, 221–224
   questions, 208–221
MySQL, 39, 53, 71, 89

N

Non-relational data, 99, 101, 133
   Azure Cosmos DB, 101
   characteristics, 99
   column-family, 102
   document, 101, 102
   graph, 102
   key-value, 101
   NoSQL data, 99
   object (Blob Storage), 102
   vs. relational, 100
   types, 101
Non-relational databases, 41
Normal Forms (NF), 65, 70
Normalization, 64, 67, 68
   Boyce-Codd Normal Form (BCNF), 68, 69
   data consistency, 65
   data redundancy, 65
   excessive normalization, 70
   Fifth Normal Form (5NF), 70
   First Normal Form (1NF), 65, 66
   Fourth Normal Form (4NF), 70

INDEX

Second Normal Form (2NF), 66, 67
Third Normal Form (3NF), 67, 68

O

OneLake, 111, 112
   AI/ML workflows, 114
   Delta Lake Foundation, 112
   enterprise-wide data sharing, 113
   features, 111, 112
   integration with Microsoft fabric tools, 114
   Logical Data Lake, 112
   real-time insights, 114
   self-service analytics, 113
   shortcuts, 113
   workspaces, 113
Online Analytical Processing (OLAP), 44
   Azure OLAP services, 45, 46
   data warehouse, 46
      BI tools, 47
      data sources, 47
      data storage, 47
      ETL, 47
      integrated, 46, 47
      non-volatile, 47
      OLAP cubes, 47
      subject oriented, 46
   drill down/up, 45
   multidimensional data, 45
   real-time querying, 45
   slice and dice, 45
Online Transaction Processing (OLTP), 42, 138
   ACID properties, 43, 44
   concurrency, 42
   data integrity, 42
   fast query execution, 43
   high transaction volume, 42
   normalization, 43
   real-time processing, 42
Open source relational databases, 89, 91
   MariaDB, 89, 90
   MySQL, 89
   PostgreSQL, 90
   See also Azure open source database services)
Optimized file formats, 37
   Avro, 37, 38
   ORC, 38
   Parquet, 38, 39
Optimized Row Columnar (ORC), 38
Oracle Database, 39
orders.txt, 32

P, Q

Parquet, 38, 39, 204
Platform-as-a-Service (PaaS), 82, 91, 161
PostgreSQL, 39, 54, 71, 90

INDEX

Power BI, 170
    benefits, 173
    capabilities and features, 184
    components, 170, 171
    data modeling, 177, 178
    interactive reports, 181, 182
    workflow
        collaborate/act, 173
        data modeling, 172
        data sources, 171
        Power Query Editor, 172
        publish/share, 173
        visualizations, 172
products.tsv, 31

R

Real-time data analytics, 137, 183–184
Real-time data stream processing, 56, 167
Relational data on azure, 62
    ACID compliance, 64
    data relationships, 62
    ER diagram for student enrollment system, 63
    explore database
        database object comparison, 80
        functions, 78
        indexes, 79
        tables, 76
        views, 77
    foreign keys, 64
    normalization, 64–68, 70
    primary keys, 63, 64
    SQL, 64, 70, 71
        command categories, 72
        DCL, 75
        DDL, 72
        DML, 74
        DQL, 73
        PL/SQL, 72
        PostgreSQL, 71
        TCL, 75
Relational database model, 62
Relational databases, 39, 40
    fundamental principles, 94, 95

S

Semi-structured data, 20, 21, 24
    data interchange, 26
    event tracking and sensor data, 26
    JSON data, 24, 25
    markers/tags, 24
    system logs, 26
    tweets, 27
    web services and APIs, 26
    XML data, 25
Spark structured streaming, 161, 166, 184
    Delta lake, 168
    ingestion, 167
    Microsoft Fabric/Azure Databricks, 169
    output, 167

INDEX

transformation, 167
use cases, 167
Speech-to-text technology, 28, 29
SQL-based systems, 21
SQLite, 39
Stakeholders, 52, 178
Structured data, 20, 21
   analytics and reporting, 23
   customer database, 22
   customer-related information, 22
   customer relationship
      management (CRM)
      system, 24
   data consistency and integrity, 23
   inventory management
      system, 22
   logistics company, 23
   SQL queries, 21
   transactional systems, 23

T

Tables
   dimension, 175
   fact, 176

Test center, 187, 188
Transactional
   workloads, 19, 42–44
Transaction Control Language
   (TCL), 75–76

U, V, W

Unstructured data, 20, 21, 27
   audio data, 28
   customer support call
      recordings, 29
   image recognition and
      classification, 28
   images and videos, 28
   sentiment analysis, 28
   text documents, 27
   voice recognition and speech-
      to-text, 28

X, Y, Z

XML data, 25
XML Schema
   Definition (XSD), 35

GPSR Compliance

The European Union's (EU) General Product Safety Regulation (GPSR) is a set of rules that requires consumer products to be safe and our obligations to ensure this.

If you have any concerns about our products, you can contact us on

ProductSafety@springernature.com

In case Publisher is established outside the EU, the EU authorized representative is:

Springer Nature Customer Service Center GmbH
Europaplatz 3
69115 Heidelberg, Germany

www.ingramcontent.com/pod-product-compliance
Lightning Source LLC
LaVergne TN
LVHW021957060526
838201LV00048B/1600